IGNACIO LARRANAGA

ENCOUNTER

Prayer Handbook

Éditions Paulines

This book originally appeared as *Encuentro*,
Ediciones Cefepal, Santiago, Chile, 1989.

Phototypesetting: *Éditions Paulines*

Cover: *Larry Mantovani*

ISBN 2-89039-570-7

Legal deposit — 4th Quarter 1992
Bibliothèque nationale du Québec
National Library of Canada

© 1992   Éditions Paulines
         250, boul. Saint-François Nord
         Sherbrooke, QC, J1E 2B9

CONTENTS

TO PRAY

FOREWORD
(To the 7th Spanish Edition)

For many years I have used the book Hymns and Prayers for the Encounters — An Experience with God. *In it were texts gleaned from many sources added to my own, texts appropriate to the atmosphere of the Encounters.*

For this book I have elaborated a series of poems and psalms appropriate for different states of mind, diverse life situations, and some other themes.

But in this new book, I have included several elements from the previous book, even though I have eliminated a substantial part of its contents. Since the authors of some of these compositions are unknown, I preferred not to mention any names.

I have included many Bible quotations, ways of praying, various exercises and practical orientations, everything abridged and simplified to its utmost. I strove to place in the hands of the reader a few simple and effective guidelines — as a Manual — to progress in the art of prayer.

Prayers written by me are the following: 1, 2, 10, 13, 15, 17, 19, 20, 21, 22, 23, 24, 25, 26, 28, 34, 36, 37, 41, 43, 45, 47, 48, 51, 53, 55, 58, 59, 60. Others belong to different authors, and some have been modified.

This edition is final and will not be altered in the future.

Ignacio Larrañaga

PRAYERS

I. THE LORD

1. Center of Gravity

To sing of you, Lord Jesus, how I wish my
eyes were an eagle, my heart of a child and
my tongue of a poet, my whole being bur-
nished by silence!

Touch my heart, Lord Jesus Christ; touch it
and you will see how the dreams concealed
in human roots since the beginning of the
world awaken.

All our voices come together at your doors.
All our waves vanish on your beaches.
All our winds sleep on your horizon.
Without knowing, the most secret desires
long after you and implore you.
The profoundest yearnings look impatiently
for you.
You are a starry night,
a diamond music, the vertex of the universe,
a fire from flint.

Where you put your wounded foot, the
planet is ablaze with blood and gold.

You walk on singing waters
and over snowy tops
you whisper in an age old forests.
You smile in the myrtle and the broom.
You breathe in algae,
mushrooms and lichen.
In the whole mineral and vegetable world I
sense you are being born, growing, living,
laughing, talking.

You are the pulse of the world, my Lord
Jesus Christ. You are the One who unceasingly comes from far away galaxies,
from the burning center of the earth,
and from the night of time;
your origin is forever,
from millions of light-years away.

On your brow shines the destiny of the
world and in your heart is concentrated the
fire of centuries.

My heart is dazzled by so many wonders,
and bowing down I say: you shall be the
King of my Territories.

For you, the fire of my blood.
You shall be my path and my light,
the cause of my joy,
the reason for my existing
and the purpose of my life,

14

my compass and my horizon,
my paragon, my wholeness
and my fulfilment.
Outside of you there is nothing for me.

My last song shall be yours.
Glory and honor are yours for ever,
King of all ages!

2. Father

How shall I call you,
you who have no name?

He came forth from the depths
of your solitude,
your son Jesus, told us
you existed and your name was *Father*.
This was the great news.

In the quiet afternoon of eternity,
when you were life and expanding fire
I lived in your mind,
you cherished me like a golden dream
and my name was written
on the palm of your right hand.
I did not deserve this
but you loved me without a reason,
you loved me as one does his only child.

From the night of my solitude
I lift my arms to tell you: Oh Love,
Father most holy, tireless sea of tenderness,
cover me with your Presence
for I am cold,
and sometimes everything frightens me.
It is said that where there is love,
there is no fear.
Why then do these black chargers
drag me towards unknown worlds
of anxiety, fear and apprehension?
Beloved Father, have mercy
and grant me the gift of peace,
the peace found when night falls.

I know you are the loving presence,
abounding, love,
infinite woodland of protection.

You are pardon and understanding,
security and certainty, joy and freedom.

I go out on the street and you are with me;
I get engrossed in work
and you remain at my side;
in agony and further on
you say to me: here I am, I go with you.

Even if I attempt to avoid your circle of love,
climb mountains or stars,
even if I were able to fly with wings of light,

all is useless...
I cannot avoid your chase.
You circle me, you submerge me
and transfigure me.

I was told your feet walked
across worlds and centuries
in search of my fleeing shadow,
and that when you found me
the sky tore open with songs.
With such good news
you have transformed me
in a prodigiously free child.
Thank you.

Now make my old castles and the high
walls of my selfishness crumble until there
is nothing left of me, not even my dust, and
thus I may be transparency for my brothers.

And then, while going through
desolate worlds,
I will also be tenderness and refuge,
I will enlighten the night of pilgrims,
I will tell orphans: "I am your mother,"
I will give shade to the exhausted,
a native land to fugitives,
and the ones who lack a home
will take shelter under my roof.

You are my home and my native land.
I wish to rest in this home
at the end of the battle.

You will certainly watch over my sleep,
Father, eternally loving and loved.
Amen.

3. Clarity

Once more, Lord, we live
a profound intimacy.
Each one of us feels his life marvelously
invaded by your life.
We are now living
the adventure of your life
in our life,
your strength in our weakness,
your vigor in our helplessness.
Your light has entered
the paths of my being.
You are light for my walking.
I know that only in your light, Lord,
will I be able to build my life beautifully.

I know you live in the light,
and that you have passed on to us
some of this light.

But unfortunately, on our part
all is darkness.

Lord, men seem
content
to walk in the dark.
They seem to like to walk as blind persons,
with a bandage over their eyes.
They do not want to see.
This also is my sin;
very often I do not want to see.

I fear that if I look at my life
I will have to change.
I implore you, Lord: open my eyes.
In this instant of honesty, I am sure,
Lord, I am certain I wish to see.
Let your light penetrate
my darkness, now.
Light, Clarity, Brightness, Blinding light.
Transparent clearness, Illuminating flash.

I want to see, Lord, I want to see. Amen.

4. You came as a friend

You reached me, humbly and discreetly,
to offer me your friendship.

You made me rise to your level,
climbing down to mine,
and you wish for a familiar relationship,
full of mutual surrender.

You remain mysteriously in me,
as an ever present friend;
you always give yourself to me,
and fulfil completely
all my aspirations.

When you give yourself to us,
with you, we possess all of creation,
since the whole universe belongs to you.
In order that our friendship be perfect,
you made me an associate
of your sufferings and joys,
you shared with me your hopes,
your projects, your life.

You invite me to share
in your work of redemption,
to put all my strength to labor with you.

You wish our friendship
to be fruitful
for myself and for others.

God, friend of man,
Creator, friend of creature,
Holy one, friend of sinner.

You are the ideal friend,
one that never fails
and never says no.

I would like to correspond to
the offering of such magnificent friendship,
the way you hope and deserve,
acting always as your friend. Amen.

5. I gave you so little

I gave you so little, Lord Jesus,
but you made it become so big!
I am so small before you,
and you make me so wise!

I did not succeed in giving you
all that I had wished,
and I did not achieve to love you
as I had wished or dreamt.

I gave you so little, truly so little,
and with such slight enthusiasm and joy.

Nonetheless, you know that in that "little"
I wanted to put all my heart.

You see the bottom of my being,
my desire to give you much more.

Since you transform my poverty in riches,
and my emptiness into plenitude,
take my whole gift as it is,
take also what it is not
so that my surrender will be full,
with my own misery,
and once more all will be created
by the supreme power of your love. Amen.

6. We need you

We need you, only you, and nothing more.
You who loves us, only you can feel all we
suffer, the compassion each one feels for
himself. Only you can measure how great a
need the world has of you, at this time.

Everyone needs you, even those who do not
know it; they need you much more than
those who know.

The hungry think they must seek bread,
while they hunger for you. The thirsty think
they need water, when they thirst for you.
The sick have unfounded hopes on finding
health; their real misfortune is your absence.
He who seeks the beauty of the world,
without knowing it, seeks you, fullness of
beauty. He who looks for truth in his

thoughts, without knowing it, longs for you, only truth worthy of knowing. He who seeks peace looks for you, the only peace where anxious hearts can rest.

They call you without knowing it, and their cry is mysteriously more distressing than ours. We need you. Come, Lord.

7. I seek your face, Lord

Leave your daily worries for a moment, insignificant man; enter for an instant within yourself withdrawing from your confused thoughts and the worries which oppress you. Rest in God only for an instant.

Enter in the depth of your soul, withdraw from everything except God and whatever can help you to find Him. Close the door of your room and look for him in silence.

Tell God with all your might, tell the Lord: I seek your face. Your face I seek, Lord.

And now, my Lord and my God, show me how and where I have to look for you, where and how I will find you.

If you are not in me, Lord, if you are absent, where will I find you? If you are everywhere why don't you make yourself present? It is true that you live in an inaccessible light, but where is that inaccessible light? How will I reach it? Who will guide me into the light so that I may contemplate you there? In what signs will I recognize you? I never saw you, my Lord and my God, I do not know your face.

God most High, what will this forsaken one do without You? What will this servant do, thirsting for your love roaming far from you? He wants to see you and your face is far away from him. He wants to be close to you and your dwelling place is inaccessible. He burns in the desire to find you and ignores where you dwell. He sighs only for you and has never seen your face.

Lord, you are my God, you are my Lord but I do not know you. You made me and you redeemed me. You asked for all I have but still I do not know you. I was made to see you and yet I have not reached the end for which I was created.

And you Lord, until when will you forget us, until when will you hide your face? When will you look toward us? When will you listen to us? When will you shine upon our eyes and show us your face? When will you answer our desires?

Lord, hear us, enlighten us, reveal yourself to us. Heed our needs, and we will be happy. Without you all is annoying and sad. Have mercy on us in our work and in the efforts we make to reach you, for without you we can do nothing.

Show me how to seek you, show me your face for, if you do not, I will not find you. I will not be able to find you unless you make yourself present. I will seek you desiring you, I will desire you as I seek you. Loving you I will find you and finding you I will love you. Amen.

8. Elevation

Oh my God, Trinity whom I adore, help me to be oblivious of myself, that I may be rooted in you, motionless and calm as though my soul were already in eternity. May nothing be able to disturb my peace nor withdraw me from you, my immutable God, but may every moment carry me further into the depths of your mystery.

Tranquilize my soul, make it your heaven, your cherished abode, and the place of your repose; may I never leave you there alone but give you my entire attention, wide awake in my faith, in state of adoration, completely surrendered to your creative action.

Oh my beloved Christ, crucified by love, may I be a bride after your own heart; may I cover you with glory and love you unto death! Yet I realize my weakness and beg you to clothe me with yourself, to identify my soul with all the movements of your heart. I beg you to embrace me, to surge up within me; to substitute yourself for me, that my life may be but a radiance of your own. Come and dwell in me as adorer, as restorer and as savior.

Oh eternal Word, expression of my God, may I spend my life listening to you; may I become completely docile that I may learn everything from you; then through all the nights and voids, in all my times of help-lessness, may I ever cling to you and dwell in your great light. Oh my beloved star, so enchant me that I can never turn from your radiance.

Oh consuming fire, Spirit of Love, descend upon me so that in my soul there may be a new incarnation of the Word, that I may be to him a new humanity wherein he renews all his mystery.

And you, Oh Father, incline yourself towards your poor creature, and overshadow him, seeing in him only your beloved Son in whom you were well pleased.

Oh my "Three", my all, my beatitude, infinite solitude, immensity wherein I lose myself, I surrender myself to you as your prey; immerse yourself in me so that I may be immersed in you, with the hope that I will contemplate in your light the depths of your greatness. Amen.

9. Invocation to the Holy Spirit

Holy Spirit, Lord of light,
from your clear celestial height,
your pure beaming radiance give.
Come, Oh Father of the poor,
come with treasures that endure,
come, Oh Light of all that live.
You of all consolers best.

And the soul's delightsome guest,
do refreshing peace bestow.
You in toil are comfort sweet,
pleasant coolness in the heat,
solace in the midst of woe.

Light immortal, light divine,
visit now this heart of mine,
and my inmost being fill.
If you take your grace away,
nothing pure in us will stay,
all our good is turned to ill.

Heal our wounds, our strength renew,
on our dryness pour your dew
wash the stains of guilt away.
Bend the stubborn heart and will,
melt the frozen, warm the chill,
guide the steps that go astray.

On all those who evermore
you confess and you adore,
in your sevenfold gifts descend.
Give them comfort when they die.
Give them life with you on high,
give them joys that never end.

II. FAITH, HOPE

10. Consolation

Lord, Lord. I can't go on anymore.
I have spent a long night;
coming out of salty waters. Be merciful.
Loneliness is a high wall
that shuts all horizons.
I lift up my eyes but I see nothing.

My brothers turned their backs on me
and left.
All of them left.
My company is my desolation;
my food is anguish.
There are no roses left, everything is mourn.
Where are you, Oh Lord?
A cruel agony is caught frozen
in the deepest part of myself.

Give me your hand, Father, hold me;
take me out of this dark prison.
Don't close the door, please, for I am alone.
Why do you remain silent?
My screams filled the night,
but you remain deaf, mute.

Awaken, my Father.
Give me a signal, at least one, that you live,
that you love me, that you are here,
now, with me.
The frightening darkness surrounds me,
it scares me,
and I only have You
as my defense.

But I know the morning will come back,
and you will comfort me again
as a mother comforts her child;
and the harmony will cover the horizons,
and rivers of consolation will flow
through my veins.

My brothers will return to my presence,
and there will be new stems and stars,
and the air will be filled with joy
and the night with songs,
and my soul will sing eternally
your mercy,
because you have consoled me.
Thank you, my Father. Amen.

11. Those who believe

Blessed are those who did not see you,
and yet believed in you.

Blessed are those who did not contemplate
your image
and proclaimed your divinity.
Blessed are those who, reading the Gospel,
have recognized in you
the One they hoped for.
Blessed are those who, in your envoys,
discerned your divine presence.

Blessed are those who,
in their innermost heart,
heard your voice and responded.
Blessed are those who,
encouraged by the desire to touch God,
have found you in mystery.
Blessed are those who,
in times of darkness,
clung more strongly to your light.

Blessed are those who,
in the hour of darkness
maintain their confidence in you.
Blessed are those who,
under the impression of your absence,
go on believing in your closeness.
Blessed are those who, not having seen you,
live in the secure hope
to see you one day. Amen.

12. Moments of obscurity

Lord Jesus Christ, out of the darkness of death you have made light arise. In the deep profoundest solitude lives, from now on and forever, the powerful protection of your love; from the obscure cover we can now sing the alleluia of those who are saved.

Grant us the humble simplicity of faith, one that does not vanish when you hound us in hours of obscurity and abandonment, when everything turns problematic.

Grant us, in these times when a mortal battle surrounds us, enough light not to lose sight of you; enough light to give to those who need it more that we do.

Make the mystery of your paschal joy shine upon us like dawn. Grant us to become real paschal people in the midst of this holy saturday of history.

Grant us that across the bright or gloomy days of our times, we may always walk with joyfulness towards the glory to come. Amen.

13. Hidden Presence

You are not there.
We cannot see your face.
You are there.
You rays burst in all directions.
You are the Hidden Presence.

Oh! presence always hidden
and always clear,
Oh! fascinating mystery
towards which concentrates
every aspiration.
Oh! intoxicating wine
that satisfies all desires.
Oh! unfathomable infinite
that soothes all delusions.

You are the Furthest and Closest of all.
Your substance dwells
in my whole being.
You bestow upon my existence
and consistency.

You penetrate me, you surround me,
you love me.

You are around me and in me.
With your active presence you reach
the remotest and deepest zones
of my privacy.

You are the soul of my soul,
the life of my life,
more me than myself,
total and totalizing reality,
in the midst of which I am submerged.
With your vivifying force
you penetrate all that I am, all that I have.

Take me entirely,
all of my all
and make me
a living transparency of your being
and of your love,
Oh! most beloved Father!

14. Lord of Victory

When all our human projects,
our earthly supports
disintegrate,
when from our most beautiful dreams
only disillusionment is left,
when our best efforts
and our firmest desires
do not reach the proposed objective,
when sincerity and loving zeal
obtain nothing,
and failure is present, distressing and cruel,
frustrating our most beautiful hopes,

you remain, Lord, indestructible
and strong,
a friend who can do everything.

Your aims remain intact,
nothing can stop
your will to come true.
Your dreams are more beautiful than ours,
and you make them come true.

You transform failure into major triumph,
you are never defeated.
You, who from sheer nothing,
make being and life arise,
you take our powerlessness
into your creative hands,
with infinite love,
and make it produce fruit, your work,
better than all our desires.

In you, our hope
is saved from disaster,
fully accomplished. Thank you. Amen.

15. God of Faith

Oh! You who have no name
and are impalpable like a shadow
but solid as a rock!
You will never be captured

through experience
nor mastered through intellectual activity,
for you are the God of faith.

> You are not something mysterious
> but mystery;
> One who cannot be
> understood analytically;
> One who will not be reduced
> to abstractions nor categories.
> One who will never be reached
> by syllogisms;
> One who is to be received,
> taken on, lived.
> One who is "understood" on our knees,
> in faith, surrendering ourselves.
> You are the God of faith.

The most excellent words of human language will never be able to confine not even a bit of your substance, they will not be able to embrace the fullness, the immensity and depth of your reality.

You surpass, contain, reach and comprise
all names and all words.
You are really the One-Without-Name,
truly the Unnamed.
You are the God of faith.

Only in the profound night of faith
when the mind is quiet,
in total silence and in the total presence,
knees bent and heart open,
only then does the certainty of faith appear,
night becomes midday, and one begins to
understand the Unintelligible.

All the while, we faintly discern your face
between semi-darkness, signs, vestiges,
analogies and comparisons.
But face to face, one cannot see you.
You are the God of faith.

Our souls long to rise up to you, to adhere
to you. We wish to possess you, to adjust
ourselves to you, and to rest. But how often
when we come close to your threshold, you
vanish like a dream, and become once more
absence and silence.

You are definitely the God of faith.

Like exiles, we are pulled towards you by
an obscure and powerful nostalgia, a
strange nostalgia for a person we have
never embraced and a native land we have
never inhabited.

You give us an appetizer and leave us without a banquet. You give us the first fruits,
but not the delight of the kingdom. You give

us a shadow, but not your face, and you leave us like a taut bow. Where are you?

Pilgrims of the Absolute and seekers of an Infinite we shall never find and since we will never "meet" you, we are destined to always walk behind you like eternal wayfarers on an odyssey that will end when we reach the ultimate shores of the native land, when faith and hope will have fallen into disuse, and only love remains. Then yes, we shall contemplate you face to face.

My God, if I am an echo of your voice, how is it that the echo continues to vibrate while the voice remains silent?
If I am thirst, and you immortal water, when will this thirst be quenched?
If I am the river, and you the sea, when will I rest in you?
I acclaim you and proclaim you,
I affirm you and confirm you,
I call for you and I need you,
I yearn for you and I long for you,
where are you?

You who have neither name nor face, in the darkness of the night,
I fall on my knees,
I surrender to you, I believe in you.

16. Prayer of Hope

Lord,
I am once again in front of your mystery.
I am constantly embraced by your presence
that so often is transformed into absence.
I look for your presence
in the absence of your presence.

When I look at the immensity of the world
I am under the impression
many have no more hope in you.
Even I make my own plans, set my goals
and lay the stones of a building
that seems to have no other architect
but me.

Nowadays, we often are
creatures who set
our hopes in our selves.
Give me, Lord,
the most profound conviction
that I will destroy my future
if hope in you
is not present.

Make me deeply understand
that in spite of the chaos of things
around me,
in spite of nights I must overcome,

in spite of the weariness of my days,
my future is in your hands
and make me see that
the earth you show me
on the horizon of the day to come
will be more beautiful and better.

I lay my steps and my days
into your mystery
for I know that your Son,
my brother,
has conquered despair
and he has guaranteed a new future
because he has risen from death to life.
Amen.

17. Suffering and redemption

Lord, what is the meaning of being a man, a woman? To suffer to one's fill. From the cries of the new-born to the last groan of the dying, suffering is the daily and bitter bread that never lacks on the family table.

My God, what good is suffering? It is a useless slough. It has no name, but it does have a thousand sources and a thousand faces, and who can avoid it? It walks by our side on the road that leads from darkness to light. What can be done with it?

It is a creature that grew out of human soil as a cursed fungus, without anyone planting it or wanting it. What can we do with it?

I remember your cross, Oh humble Jesus of Nazareth; you did not choose this cross, but you took it on, most certainly with peace. Of what use is this vast current of human suffering? That is the question: what can be done with this essential and burning mystery?

Thousands of disabilities, hordes of misunderstandings, of intimate conflicts, of nervous breakdowns and obsessions, of resentments and envies, of melancholy and sadness, of limits and helplessness, our own and that of others, the pain, the nails, the torture... Of what use can this endless forest of dead leaves be?

You, the just one, the obedient and submissive servant of the Father, when your hour came, after you quivered with fear, you surrendered yourself peacefully and you freely accepted to drain the cup of sorrow to the bitter end. Actions of human conspiracy did not fall upon you blind and fatal, but you took them on voluntarily. Knowing that they were not a human intrigue, but because the Father permitted them. You took your cross with love.

I thank you for the instruction, Christ, my friend. We now have the answer to the fundamental question of man: what can be done with suffering?

Suffering is not conquered by complaining, by fighting it or by resisting, but by taking it on. When we take on our cross lovingly, not only do we accompany you, Jesus of Nazareth, on the road to Calvary, but we cooperate with you in the redemption of the world, and much more, "we make up for what is lacking to the passion of the Lord".

Perfect freedom is not only to take on the cross with love, but to be grateful for it, knowing that in this manner we take on human suffering and we participate in the transcendent task of redeeming humanity.

I thank you, Lord Jesus Christ, for the wisdom of the cross.

III. CIRCUMSTANCES

18. Morning Prayer

Lord, in the silence of this new day,
I open the door to peace.
I come to ask you for peace,
wisdom and strength
which come from you.
Today, I want to look at the world with eyes
filled with love;
I want to be patient,
understanding, humble, meek and good.
To see your sons beyond
their outward appearance,
as you see them yourself,
in order to appreciate
the kindness of each one.
Close my ears to idle words,
keep my tongue from slander,
that I may only have
thoughts of blessing.
I want to be so well-intentioned and just
that all who approach me
may feel your presence.
Clothe me, Lord, with your goodness,

and all through this day,
may I be a reflection of you. Amen.

19. Plea for the Night

My father, now that voices have hushed and
that cries have ceased, my soul rises to you
to say: I believe in you, I hope in you, I love
you with all my might. Glory to you, Lord.

I commit into your hands the fatigue and
the battle, the joys and the disappointments
of this day which has ended.

If my nerves betrayed me, if self-centered
impulses had the best of me, if I allowed
resentment or melancholy invade me, forgive me, Lord. Have mercy on me.

If I have been unfaithful, if my mouth spoke
idle words, if I let myself be overcome by
impatience, if I was a thorn for someone,
forgive me, Lord. I do not want to fall asleep
without feeling in my soul the safety of your
mercy, Lord, sweet and unbinding.

I give you thanks, my Father, for you were
the refreshing shadow that shielded me all
through the day. I give you thanks because
all along these hours, you surrounded me

— invisible, affectionate — you watched over me like a mother.

Lord, around me all is silent and calm. Send the angel of peace over this house. Relax my nerves, appease my spirit, set my mind at rest, flood my being with silence and serenity.

Watch over me, beloved Father, when I surrender to sleep, confident as a child happily sleeps in your arms.

In your name, Lord, I will rest peacefully. Amen.

20. Prayer During Sickness

A Prayer for Health to you Lord, who passed through this world healing all sickness and pain, I cry out to you; as a poor tree scourged by pain, Son of David, have mercy on me.

My health is failing as a statue of sand. I am enclosed in a fatal circle; the hospital, the bed, the tests, the diagnostics, the alcohol, the cotton, the nurse, I cannot leave that circle. I feel a beast in the innermost part of my body and no one finds it. Have mercy on me, Lord.

My God, every morning I am tired when I awake, my eyes are red from sleeplessness. I often feel as heavy as a bag of sand. My bones feel eaten away, my insides torn, and as a mad dog, pain gnaws me and above all I fear, Lord.

I am very frightened. Fear as a wet garment clings to my soul. What will become of me? Will the down of health come upon me? Will I some day be able to sing the glory of the healed?

My God, when will you visit me? Did you not say: "Arise and Walk"? Did you not say to Lazarus "Come out"? Did not the lepers heal and the lame walk at the command of your voice? Did you not order: "Let go of the crutches", "Walk on Water"? When will my hour come? When may I also sing your wonders? Son of David have mercy on me, You are my only hope.

And yet I know there is something worse than sickness: anxiety. Health is good but peace is still better. What good is health without peace? And what I need, most of all is peace, my Lord Jesus Christ. Anxiety, dark shadow of loneliness, fear and uncertainty, anguish assaults me and at times, totally dominates me. Frequently I feel sadness, and at times, deathly sadness.

I need peace, Lord Jesus, that peace that you alone can give. Give me peace which is consolation, that peace which is the fruit of total surrender. Therefore I place my health in the hands of the physicians and I will do all that is possible to regain it. The rest I leave in your hands.

From this moment, I let go of the oars and leave my boat to drift in the divine currents.

Take me wherever you wish, Lord. Give me health and long life. May it not be as I desire but as you wish.

I know tonight you will console me. Fill me with your serenity, that is all I ask. Amen.

21. Unity in Marriage

Lord, one day on the bare ground
suddenly appeared
a flower of snow and fire.

This flower stretched a golden bridge
between two banks,

garland that joined forever
our lives and our fate.
Lord, such was love and its prodigies,
rivers, emeralds and illusions.
Glory to you, incandescent furnace of love!

And time passed,
and in the confused splendor of the years
the garland lost its freshness,
and frost
encircled the flame;
shadowed the routine,
curse invaded our lives,
without us being aware.
And love began to hibernate.

Lord, fountain of love,
on our knees
we offer you our fervent plea;
Be light and fire in our home,
bread, rock, dew
and backbone.
May wounds be dressed every night
and each morning love rise again
like a renewed spring.
Without you our dreams will be scattered.
Be for us faithfulness,
cheerfulness, and stability.

Maintain in our home, Lord,
high as the stars,

the blaze of love
and may unity, as a bounteous river,
travel through our arteries
day after day.

Be, Lord, the golden link
that keeps our lives
incorruptibly intertwined
till the last confines and beyond. Amen.

22. A child is born

He is here,
and the house is full of fragrance.
One would think spring is here.
In you, Father most holy,
bounteous source of all fatherhood,
in you are all our sources.
You have sent us a present
longed for and dreamt of;
a child has joined our banquet.
Welcome.

What words could tell of our gratitude,
Lord of life?
Thank you for his eyes and his hands,
thank you for his feet and his skin,
thank you for his body and his soul.

We put him in your hands
filled with tenderness:
please do watch over him, and cuddle him
and fill him with sweetness.

Beloved Father, most holy One,
assign an angel
to guide this child
on the road to health and comfort,
to make him mindful of your voice.

And may Good, Peace and Blessings
be with this child all the days of his life.
Amen.

23. A Happy Home

Lord Jesus, you lived in a happy family.
Make this house the abode of your presence,
a warm and joyful home.
Send peace upon all its members,
serenity upon our nerves,
control upon our tongues,
health upon our bodies.

May our children be loved
and may they sense it,
and may ingratitude and greed
be banned away from them.
Lord, overwhelm the heart of the parents

with patience and understanding
and with unlimited generosity.

Lord God, extend a tent of love
to protect and refresh,
to warm and to mature
all the children of the house.

Give us our daily bread
and banish from our house
the need to show off,
to shine and to be seen;
free us from the vanities of the world
and from ambitions which make us uneasy
and steal our peace.

May joy shine in our eyes,
may confidence open all doors,
may happiness radiate like the sun
and may peace be queen of this home.
We ask this of you,
you who were a happy son
in your home of Nazareth,
close to Mary and Joseph.

24. Good News

At dawn a messenger came
and in the afternoon the letter carrier.
And the house was filled with light.

Our fears ceased to exist.
And we were able to breathe again.
The most optimistic calculations
were surpassed.

Harmony returned.
Success smiled.
Health regained.

The good news of the afternoon
filled us with peace.
Smiles reappeared on our lips.
We are happy.

My God, let me say:
sheaves of grain and mountain peaks,
snow and rivers,
give thanks to the Lord. Amen.

25. Requiem for a Cherished One

Silence and peace.
He was taken to the land of life.
Why ask questions?
His home, for now, is rest,
and his clothing, light. Forever.
Silence and peace. What do we know?

My God, Lord of history and master of days
gone by and of tomorrow, in your hands lie

the keys of life and of death. Without asking us questions, you have taken him to your holy dwelling, and we close our eyes, we bow our head and we simply say: Amen.

Silence and peace.

The music of life has been submerged in deep waters and nostalgia rests in boundless prairies.

The battle is over. He will no longer know tears or grasps. The sun will forever shine upon him, and peace will determine his boundaries.

Lord of life and master of our destinies, in your hands we silently place our dearly beloved who has left us.

While we entrust to the soil his passing remains, may his immortal soul live eternally in unending peace, in your loving bosom, Father of mercy.

Silence and peace.

IV. STATE OF MIND

26. A Prayer When in Fear

Lord, there are clouds in the horizon
and the sea is in a fury.
I am frightened!

Fear paralyzes my blood.
Invisible hands pull me back,
I have no courage!

A flock of dark birds is crossing
the firmament.
What is this?

My God, tell my soul "I am your victory."

Repeat within me.
"Do not fear, I am with you."

27. Peace

Lord, fill my heart with hope
and my lips with sweetness!
Fill my eyes with the light
that embraces and purifies.

Mark my hands with a forgiving touch.
Give me courage in my struggles,
compassion when offended,
mercy in ungratefulness and injustice.

Deliver me from envy
and from petty ambition,
from hatred and vengeance,
and as I return tonight to my rest,
may I feel your presence within me.

Amen.

28. Times of Depression

My God, my God, why have you forsaken
me? I feel as if a brick wall had unexpect-
edly collapsed on me. I do not know where
to run and I do not want to live. Where are
you, Lord?

Wretched, in a waste land, I can only see
shadows around me. Where can I go?
God, have mercy.

Poor wingless angel! Forsaken on ignored
and misty roads. Where am I? I am at the
bottom of the sea and I cannot breathe.
Where is the light? Does the sun still shine?

Worse than emptiness and a thing of naught, what is the horror of simply being human? My God, why do you not delete me from the role of the living?

Like a besieged city, anguish, dejection, bitterness and torment encircle me and suffocate me. What is this called? Nausea? Aversion of life? Desolation stretches its grey wings from one horizon to the next. Where is the way out? Is there no exit? You alone are my refuge, my God.

I do not forget, Jesus, Son of God and Servant of the Father, that at Gethsemane, under the shadows of the olive trees and in the moonlight, tedium and agony made you shed tears and blood; and I remember that an intense and deadly sadness flooded your inner being like a bitter sea. But everything passed.

I know that my night shall also pass. I know you will tear this darkness, my God, and that tomorrow solace will awaken. The massive barriers will collapse and I shall breathe once more. Tomorrow my poor soul will be cared for and I shall live anew.

And I shall say: thank you my God, because this was all a nightmare; the bad dream of a night that now belongs to the past. Meanwhile, give me patience and hope. Your will be done, my God. Amen.

29. Gratitude

Even if our lips were filled with songs
like the sea,
and our tongue filled with joy
like the lap of its waves,
our lips overflowing with praise
like the infinity of the firmament,
and even if our eyes glow
like the sun and the moon,
and our arms stretch out
like an eagle into space,
and our feet are as weightless
as deers'...

We could not begin to thank you, Adonai, our God and God of our fathers, nor to bless your name for a tiny part of what you have accomplished for our forefathers and for us. Amen.

30. Forgive me, Lord

If, exhausted, I fall in the middle of the road,
forgive me, Lord.
If one day my heart staggers at the thought
of suffering,
forgive me, Lord.

Forgive my weakness.
Forgive me for hesitating.

The splendid garland
I offered to God this morning
is already withering;
its beauty vanishes.
Forgive me, Lord.

V. SELF-SURRENDER

31. Act of Self-Surrender

In your hands, Oh God, I abandon myself.
Mold this clay as does the potter.
Give it shape and afterward,
if you so wish, break it.
Command, order,
"What do you want me to do?
What do you want me to avoid?"

Praised or humiliated, persecuted,
misunderstood or slandered,
comforted, hurt, useless,
the only thing for me to say,
following your Mother's example, is
"Let it be done unto me
according to your word."

Give me love, above all things
love of the cross.
Not of a heroic cross
that would satisfy my ego
but of the humble everyday crosses which I
shoulder reluctantly.
Give me the love of the crosses

I encounter each day
in contradiction, in neglect, in failure,
in erroneous judgments and in indifference;
in rebuff and contempt from others,
in discomfort
and in sickness, in intellectual limitations
and in barrenness, in the silence of the heart.

Only then will you know that I love you,
even though
I may not know it myself. But that will do.
Amen.

32. Surrender

The road that leads to a friend
is never too long,
nor too small the place
where he lives.
If generous individuals
follow the road which leads to you
and earnestly request of you
the gifts of the spirit,
one after another...

We, on the contrary,
leave our mounts
in total surrender to your will,
and refuse to continue

the journey in which we stop unceasingly,
to start anew.
We leave our impediments
before your door.

My God, we entrust to you
all our interests, without exception.

Dispose of them as you wish;
do not let us go back to our own securities
God of majesty! Amen.

33. Prayer of Self-Surrender

My Father,
I surrender myself to you:
do with me what you will.
Whatever you do
I thank you for it.

I am ready for everything,
and I accept everything,
provided that your will be done in me
and in all your creatures.
I desire nothing else, Oh my God.

I entrust my soul into your hands.
I give it to you, my God,
with all the love of my heart,
because I love you,

and it is a necessity of love for me
to give myself, to entrust myself
into your hands without measure,
with infinite confidence,
for you are my Father. Amen.

34. Patience

Son,
if you seriously venture on the road of God,
prepare your soul for the trials
that will occur,
sit patiently before his doorstep,
calmly accepting the silence,
absence and delays
to which he will submit you,
for gold is refined in the heart.

Lord Jesus, since you lived among us
clothed with patience as a distinctive sign,
patience is the queen of virtues
and the most precious gem of your crown.

Give me the grace to accept peacefully
the essential gratuity of God,
the bewildering road of grace
and the unpredictable emergencies
of nature.
I calmly agree to

the slow and staggering stride of prayer
and I accept that the road to holiness
be so long and difficult.

I accept with peace
life's displeasures
and my brothers' lack of understanding,
sickness and death itself,
and the law of human insignificance,
that is to say that after my death
all will continue as if nothing
had happened.

I peacefully accept the fact of wanting
so much and being capable of so little
and that with great efforts
I will only obtain minimal results.
I peacefully accept the law of sin, that is:
I do what I do not want
and I do not do what I would like.
In peace, I leave in your hands
what I should have been and was not
and what I should have done and did not.

I accept in peace all human incapacities
which surround me and restrict me.
I peacefully accept the law of perils
and of what is provisional,
the law of mediocrity and of failure,
the law of solitude and of death.

In exchange for this surrender,
Lord, give me peace.

35. Take me

Take me, Lord Jesus,
take me with all that I am
with all that I have and all that I achieve,
what I think and what I live.
Take my spirit
so that it may cling to you
in the intimacy of my heart
and love only you.

My God, take me in my secret desires,
so that they may be my dreams
and my ultimate goal,
my total attachment and
my perfect happiness.

Take me with your goodness,
attracting me to you.
Take me with your gentleness,
accepting me in you.
Take me with your love,
uniting me to you.
Take me my Savior in your suffering,
your joy, your life, your death,

in the night of your cross,
in the everlasting day of your resurrection.

Take me with your power, lifting me to you;
take me with your fire, to set me ablaze;
take me with your greatness,
so that I may lose myself in you.

Take me for the work of your great mission,
so that I may surrender myself totally for
the salvation of my fellow-men and women
and for any sacrifice at the service
of your brothers and sisters.

Take me, Oh Christ, my God,
without limitations and without end.
Take whatever I can offer you;
never give me back what you have taken,
so that one day
I may possess you in heaven,
hold you and keep you forever. Amen.

36. Hymn of Surrender

My Father,
today I lift my voice to sing to you
for instead of daylight,
in lieu of sun with its light and colors,
you have left me in darkness,
in the cold nights.

I love you,
I adore you
because the waves of the sea of your might
have flooded and destroyed
my dreams and my castles;
they have undone the sweetest,
the strongest,
the most sacred links of my existence.

I love you,
I adore you and I bless you
because instead of the warmth
of your tenderness
the coldness of indifference
entered my garden freezing the last flower.

Lord, my God,
I bless you and praise you
for in your most holy will
you have permitted the shadows of dusk
to fade the richness of my youth;
because you wanted me to be not
a star nor a brilliant and lovely chalice
but plain and trivial sand
in the vast beach of humanity.

If one day I praised you in joy
and sang of you in the heart of this light
through which you have transfigured
my life,

today I love you and I adore you
in the shadow of the cross.

I bless you in difficulty and in work,
amidst the stones and the ruggedness
of the ascent;
and the tears I shed today
fall from my grateful soul
that blessed you in tedium and poverty
in the gray shadows of sadness
because in spite of it all
you gave me affectionately
this blue and infinite vault
to shroud, Lord, my misfortune.

Yet, kiss affectionately and in self-surrender
these divine hands that hurt me,
because I firmly believe that
neither one hair nor one leaf
drops without the loving will of the Father
who widely conducts
the orchestra of the universe.

Yes, powerful and beloved Father,
from deep within,
my astonished and grateful soul
praises you,
and I exult in a song of hope.
If one day you change my plans,
if for one moment you put out my flame,
it is because,

beyond the glistening of objects,
of perfumes, of flowers that wither,
I catch sight of a world,
different and more beautiful,
of a country where the sun does not set
and of a luminous house
built on eternal peace.
I place myself in your hands;
do with me what you will. Amen.

VI. TRANSFORMATION

37. The Grace of Fraternal Love

Lord Jesus,
it was your great dream:
that we be one as the Father
and You are one and that our unity
be fulfilled in your unity.

It was your great commandment, your last
will and distinctive banner for those who
follow you: that we love one another as you
had loved us; and you loved us as the
Father had loved you. That was the source
and measure of the model.

With the twelve you made a family of pilgrims. You were truthful and sincere with
them, demanding and understanding but
most of all, you were very patient.
Just as in a family,
you warned them against dangers,
you encouraged them
at times of difficulties,
you rejoiced with their success,
you washed their feet,

you served them at the table.
You first gave us the example
and then you gave us the command:
love one another as I have loved you.

In the new family or fraternity which we make up today, you are a gift from the Father and we accept you as our brother. Lord Jesus, You will be the strength which binds us and our joy.

If you are not alive among us, this community will collapse like an artificial structure.

You duplicate yourself and become alive in each member and for this reason, we strive to respect each other as we would respect you; and your presence will question us when unity and peace are threatened in our midst. We, therefore, ask that you remain very much alive within our hearts.

Remove from between us the high walls of selfishness, pride and vanity. Keep away from our doors the envies which obstruct and destroy unity. Deliver us of inhibitions. Calm aggressive impulses. Purify our original sources. And allow us to feel as you felt and to love as you loved. You will be our model and guide, Oh Lord Jesus.

Give us the grace of fraternal love: may a sensible, warm and deep current run through our relationships; may we understand and forgive each other; may we encourage and enjoy each other as sons and daughters of the same mother. Do not allow in our path obstacles, withdrawals nor blockages but rather may we all be open, loyal, sincere and loving so that trust may grow as a shady tree covering us all, brothers and sisters in a home, Lord Jesus Christ.

Thus we will achieve a warm, happy home which will rise as a city on a mountain, as a prophetic sign that your Great Dream has been attained and that you, Lord Jesus, are alive among us. Amen.

38. Decision

Oh Christ,
I am in the darkness,
and the darkness hurts
and injures me.
I miss you.
I know you are in me.
But you are quiet, still
awaiting my decision.

You know...
I cannot live without you.
Life without you is empty,
it has no meaning,
it is colorless
It is agony.

Oh Christ,
do not stay silent.
Save me!

39. Complete conversion

I know you are asking something of me,
Lord Jesus.
So many doors open at once,
my life is before my eyes,
not as in a dream.

I know you expect something of me, Lord,
and here I am
at the foot of the wall: everything is open,
there is only one free road,
open to the infinite, to the absolute.

But in spite of everything,
I have not changed.
I will seek you Lord
for a long time still.
To die, but this time, for good.

Like the wounded who suffer, Lord,
I ask that you put an end to my struggle.
I am tired of not belonging to you
and of not being yours.

40. Detain

How good it is to pause!
Lord, I would like to slow down
right now.
Why so much commotion?
Why so much frenzy?
I do not know how to stop.
I have forgotten to pray.
Now I close my eyes, and
I wish to talk to you, Lord.
I wish to open to your universe,
but my eyes cannot bear to be kept closed.
I feel a frantic agitation
invade my whole body,
it comes and goes, prisoner of haste.
Lord, I would like to stop right now.
Why such a hurry?
Why such unrest?
I cannot save the world.

I am barely a drop of water
in the immense ocean
of your marvellous creation.

What is really important,
is to seek your presence.
What is really important
is to stop from time to time,
and to proclaim
your greatness,
your beauty, your splendor,
and that you are love.
What is urgent, is to listen to you
and to let you speak within me,
live in the depth of things
and to constantly take time
to look for you in the silence
of your mystery.

My heart continues to beat,
but in a different way,
I am doing nothing
I am not hurrying
I am simply before you, Lord.
And how good it is to be before you. Amen.

41. The grace of humility

Lord Jesus, meek and humble.

From the dust I feel controlled by this unquenchable thirst to be admired, the need to

be loved by others oppresses me. My heart is full of impossible dreams.

I crave for redemption.
My God, have mercy.

I just cannot forgive,
resentment consumes me,
criticism hurts me,
failure devastates me,
rivalry frightens me.

My heart is conceited. Give me the grace of humility, my Lord, gentle and meek of heart.

I do not know the origin of this insane appetite to impose my will, to eliminate any rival, to consent to vengeance. I do what I do not want to do. Have mercy, Lord, and give me the grace of humility.

Enormous chains enwrap my heart; this heart subdues and takes over all that I am and all that I do, everything that surrounds me. And these appropriations generate so many fears in me. Poor me, owner of myself, who will break my chains? Your grace, my poor and humble Lord. Give me the grace of humility.

The grace to forgive with all my heart. The grace to accept criticism and contradiction or at least, to doubt myself when I am corrected.

Give the grace of self-criticism.

The grace to remain undisturbed by scorn, neglect and indifference; to feel happiness in being unknown; to not encourage feelings, words and actions of self-satisfaction.

Lord, open free spaces in me so that they may be filled by you and my brothers and sisters.

Then, my Lord Jesus Christ, give me the grace to acquire a heart unattached and open like yours; a meek and patient heart. Christ Jesus, gentle and meek, make my heart like yours. Amen.

42. Before your face, Lord

I have looked for you Lord, as much as I could, as much as you allowed me. I have done my utmost to understand with my intellect what I believed through faith; in discussions I became extremely tired.

Lord, My God, my only hope, listen to me so that I may not become disheartened and cease to seek you. I have always searched to see your face. Give me strength for the quest. You allowed me to find you and gave me the hope of a better understanding. Before you, are my strength and my feebleness; keep the first and heal the latter. Before you, are my wisdom and my ignorance. If you open your door, welcome those who enter and if you close it, open for those who knock insistently.

Make me remember you, make me understand you and love you. Make these gifts grow in me until the moment I surrender completely to you. Amen.

43. The grace of mutual respect

Jesus Christ, our Lord and our brother,
place a bolt on the door of our heart
so that it may not think evil of anyone,
judge unfavorably,
make false assumptions or misinterpret,
so that we may not invade
the sacred sanctuary of intentions.

Lord Jesus, unifying link of our fraternity, put a seal of silence on our lips in order to block any murmuring or unfavorable comment, to zealously keep confidences until death, knowing that the first and most perfect way to love is to keep silence.

Make us kind and understanding. Give us a spirit of courtesy so that we may have for one another the consideration we would have for you. And at the same time, give us the necessary wisdom to surround this courtesy with fraternal trust.

Lord Jesus Christ, give us the grace
to respect one another. Amen.

44. Lead me

Guide me, radiant light
through the darkness that surrounds me,
always take me further on.
This night is dark
and I am far from home,
guide me further on.

Guide my steps: I do not ask
to see right away
what you have in store for me in the future.
One step at a time is sufficient

for the time being.
I was not always like this;
and I have not always prayed
for you to lead me.
I preferred to choose my own way;
but now I pray that you guide me.
I dreamt of days of glory
and pride lead my steps.
I pray: do not remember those past years.

Your might has abundantly blessed me;
and undoubtedly today
you will lead me through mounts and vales,
through stony paths and steep ridges
until night ends
and morning smiles.
Tomorrow, the faces of angels
I loved for so long
but have lost sight of,
will smile again.

Guide me, radiant light,
take me further on. Amen.

45. The Grace of Dialogue

Lord God, we praise you and glorify you for
the beauty of the gift named *dialogue*. It is a
favorite child of God for it is like a stream

gushing unceasingly within the Holy Trinity.

Dialogue unties knots,
dissipates suspicions,
opens doors,
resolves conflicts,
makes the person greater,
is bond of unity
and "mother" of brotherhood.

Christ Jesus, unity of the gospel community, make us realize that our lack of understanding is almost always due to a lack of dialogue.

Make us understand that dialogue is neither an argument nor a battle of ideas, but a search of the truth between two or more people. Make us understand that we need each other, and that we complement each other: we have something to give and a need to receive, I can see what others cannot, and they can see what I do not.

Lord Jesus, when tension builds up, give me humility so that I may not want to impose my truth by attacking my brother's truth; make me keep silent when necessary; make me wait for the other person to completely finish expressing his truth.

Give me wisdom to understand that no human being is able to totally possess the truth and that no error nor tactlessness is without some truth.

Give me common sense to recognize that I can also be mistaken on one or another aspect of truth; let me be enriched by the other person's truth. Finally, give me the generosity to understand that the other person also honestly seeks the truth and to look without prejudice and with kindness at the opinion of others. Lord Jesus, give me the grace to dialogue. Amen.

46. Transfiguration

Lord, again we are together.
Together, you and I,
and you and my brothers and sisters.
Your life has entered my life.

My history is so trite, so empty,
so common.
I do not even have a history.

Sometimes I wonder
if my life has any meaning.
So much emptiness, so many complications,
so much unfaithfulness!

But when I am with you,
it is as if enthusiasm
and energy came back to life.

And today with my brothers
Peter, James and John, I saw
your face transfigured,
glowing.
You, Lord Jesus, are the God of all light.
You are the God of brightness and beauty.

It is good to be close to you,
it is good to live with you.
But Lord, it is even better
to know that you are with me
throughout my life,
by your grace, by your love.
It is good to know
that my face
will also be transfigured,
glowing, as
you transform me.

Freely, cheerfully
I beseech you with joy, that I may
be more and more identified with you,
to the point of saying
with the apostles;
"Master, it is good to be here!"

47. The grace of communicating

Lord Jesus,
you have called the disciples "friends"
because you revealed your innermost self
to them.
How hard it is to open oneself, Lord!
How difficult it is to tear apart
the veil of one's own mystery.

How many obstacles are on the road!
But I know very well, Lord,
that without communication
there is no love,
and that the essential mystery of fraternity
consists of unveiling and of welcoming
one another.

Make me understand, Lord,
that I was created
not as a finished and closed being
but to grow and move
towards others;
that I must share in the richness of others
and let others share in my rightness,
that to close oneself is death,
and to open oneself is life,
freedom, maturity.

Lord Jesus Christ, king of fraternity,
give me the confidence and the courage
to open myself to others,
teach me the art of unveiling myself.
Destroy in me shyness and fear,
barriers and restraints
that are obstacles to the flow
of communication.
Give me generosity to spring forward
without fear
in the enriching game of opening
and welcoming.

Lord Jesus,
give us the grace of communication.

VII. APOSTOLIC WORK

48. In the light of your presence

Lord Jesus,
may your presence overwhelm my being,
and your likeness be engraved
in my heart,
so that I may walk in the light of your face,
think as you thought,
feel as you felt,
behave the way you behaved,
talk as you talked
dream as you dreamt,
and love as you loved.

That I may, like you,
forget myself in order to
attend to others,
insensitive to myself
and compassionate towards others;
to sacrifice myself, and be at the same time
encouragement and hope for others.

That I may, like you
be sensitive and merciful,
patient, meek and humble,

genuine and true.
That your favorite, the poor,
may also be my favorite;
your goals become my goals.
That seeing me, others may see you.
And that I may become transparency
of your being and of your love. Amen.

49. Prayer for action

Lord, give us the wisdom
that judges from above and that sees afar.
Give us the spirit that omits
the irrelevant in favor of the essential.
Teach us serenity
in times of confrontation and obstacles,
and to progress in faith without agitation
along the road laid out by you.
Give us peace so that
we may embrace everything
with a vision of unity.

Help us to accept criticism
and contradiction.
Let us avoid
disorder and dispersion.

With you, may we love all things.
Oh God, source of being, unite us to you

and to everything that leads us
to happiness and eternity. Amen.

50. You are with us

You are with us every day
until the end of the world.

You are with us, divine Omnipotence
with our frailties.

You are with us, infinite love,
who accompanies us on our way.

You are with us, supreme protection
and guaranteed triumph over temptation.

You are with us, energy that supports
our hesitant generosity.

You are with us
in our struggles and our failures,
in our difficulties and our trials.

You are with us
in our disappointments and our anxieties,
to give us back courage.

You are with us in sadness
to communicate the enthusiasm
of your joy.

You are with us in solitude
like an unwavering friend.

You are with us
in our apostolic mission
to guide and sustain us.

You are with us
to lead us to the Father
on the road of wisdom
and eternity. Amen.

51. Solidarity

You were the first, Christ Jesus, while relin-
quishing the glory of divinity, to become
one with man, poor pilgrim bearing this
solitude. You became part of the caravan of
human existence to its ultimate conse-
quences.

Bind me to others so that
I may walk with the crippled,
lend a hand to the blind,
assist those who die abandoned in hospitals,
teach reading and writing to the illiterate,
        share my house with the homeless,
        evicted for not paying rent,
give help to whomever has an extreme
    emergency,

protest for those who have been tortured or
massacred for defending the oppressed,
take the bread from my mouth to give it to
the hungry dying on the road,
attend funerals of those who died in factory
accidents, the scaffold, in any field of
work or those who fell in the street,
riddled with bullets by agents of re-
pression.
Take the place of one who has raised his
voice in favor of the oppressed,
be part of the march of those who fight for
human rights, for unity of workers, for
better wages, for brotherly understanding, for justice and for peace.

They will all sit at your right, Lord, haloed
by the beatitudes; the persecuted for justice,
and those who worked for peace.

52. Supplication

Give me, Lord, the candor of a child
and the conscience of an adult.
Give me, Lord, the caution of an astronaut
and the courage of a rescuer.
Give me, Lord, the humbleness of a sweeper
and the forbearance of the sick.

Give me, Lord, the idealism of youth
and the wisdom of elders.
Give me, Lord, the availability
of the Good Samaritan
and the gratitude of the needy.
Give me, Lord, all the good I see
in my brothers and sisters,
whom you have overwhelmed
with your gifts.

Lord, let me imitate your saints,
or better still, make me
what you want me to be:
persevering like a fisherman,
full of hope
like a christian.
Let me stay on the path of your Son
and at the service of my brothers and sisters.
Amen.

53. Generosity

Lord, teach me how to be generous,
to give without speculating,
to repay evil with good,
to serve without expecting a reward,
to get close to the one who least please me,
to do good to those who cannot repay me,

to love always freely,
to work without seeking rest.

And not having anything else than to give,
to give myself always more
to whomever needs me,
expecting the reward from you alone.
Or better still: hoping you,
yourself, will be my reward.
Amen.

54. Where are you?

I beseech you, Lord, that I may one day
hear the song of men and women
who have found love,
the day they will have forgotten hatred,
wars, races, colors.

One day, I hope to see a new world
rediscover its faith in you.

For you alone can fulfil
the emptiness felt by the world.

I also look for you.
Where are you?
Where... Where are you?
When night falls upon earth,
I turn to you.

But the stars do not answer
my questions.

I know you are my brother.
I know the voice of my brothers is yours.
I know your skin is of every color.
I know you speak every language.
I know you are in all nations.
I know your name knows no limit
of time or space.

I have looked for you, and now I know
where you are. Amen.

55. The gift of work

Since early childhood, Lord Jesus,
in the shop of an artisan,
you earned your bread
by the sweat of your brow.
Since then, work acquired a divine nobility.

Through work, we are transformed
into companions and cooperators of God
and into craftsmen of our history.
Work is the anvil where man shapes
his maturity and his grandeur,
the flour of which daily bread is made.

Matter passing through the hands of men,
is transformed into a vehicle of love.
Make me understand, Lord,
the love of those who erect shelters,
those who sow grain,
those who sweep streets, build houses,
repair damages,
listen to problems or simply study
for tomorrow's labor and service.

Give us, Lord, the grace to offer you
the day's labor
as a liturgical gesture, as a living mass
for your glory and the service
of our brothers. Amen.

56. Word and fire

Father, fountain of light and warmth, send us your living word; let us greet it without fear and let us be embraced by it.

Let your word come, Lord, and when our hearts are aflame with your unquenchable fire, we will transmit this fire to one another.

Transform us, Lord, into warm and glowing words, able to set the world on fire, so that each person may feel wrapped in the infinite flames of your love. Amen.

57. We pray to you, Lord

Lord God, we ask you to bless the honest work done in fields and factories; in schools, offices and stores; in any place where we earn our daily bread for the development of arts and science.

And since you commanded man to submit the forces of creation and to master them, lead us by the hand, Lord, so that we may use natural energies, especially the ones over which we have some control, for the good of people and not for their destruction, thanking you, Lord and creator of all the forces of the universe.

Since you have given us such a marvellous power, make all men, our brothers, recognize you in Jesus Christ, Lord and Redeemer of all creatures, and may we serve you with a deep sense of responsibility in each of the actions we undertake.

Have mercy on men and women who do not have hope, and on those who, day after day, experience only suffering. Lord, we implore you: stay with us, through your word, by your grace and by the solace of the Holy Spirit. In the name and by the merits

of Jesus Christ, savior and hope of the
world. Amen.

58. Option for the poor

Lord Jesus, brother of the poor,
before the dubious glitter of the powerful
you stripped yourself of your power.

From the heights of divinity
you came down towards man and touched
his abyss.
Being all richness you became poverty.
Being the center of the world,
you became the outskirts,
limited and captive.

You left aside the rich and the satisfied
and you took the torch
of the oppressed and the forsaken,
and you stood by their side.
Lifting high the banner of mercy,
you walked through mounts and vales
searching for the injured sheep.

You said the rich already had their God
and that only the poor leave
space for amazement;
the land and the kingdom,

the field and the harvest will be theirs.
Blessed are they!

It is time to fold our tents and move on
to stop misfortune and lament,
to break chains
and to maintain the struggle for dignity,
so that the dawn of liberation
may come at last
when swords are buried
in the fertile soil.

There are many poor, Lord; they are legions.
Their hue and cry bursts, grows, impetuous
and sometimes threatening
like a swelling storm.

Give us, Lord Jesus, your sensitive
and daring heart;
free us from indifference and passivity;
enable us to get involved,
to also take a stand
for the poor and destitute.

Time has come to collect the banners
of righteousness and of peace,
to deeply get involved in the crowds
between tension and conflict,
and to defy materialism
with alternative solutions.

Give us, king of the poor,
wisdom to weave a single garland
with these two red flowers;
contemplation and combat.
And give us the crown of the beatitudes.
Amen.

59. To serve

Oh Christ, to better serve you
give me a noble heart.
A heart that is strong
to aspire for great ideals
and not for mediocre options.

A heart that is generous at work,
seeing it not as an imposition
but rather as a mission you entrust me.

A heart that is noble in suffering,
being a brave soldier before my own cross,
helping others to carry theirs.

A heart that is open to the world,
understanding its frailty
but immune to its maxims and seductions.

A heart that is great
towards men and women,
loyal and attentive towards all,

but especially obliging and dedicated
towards the poor and the humble.

A heart that is never self-centered,
always depending on you,
happy to serve you
and to serve my brethren,
my Lord,
all the days of my life. Amen.

VIII. MARY

60. Lady of Silence

Mother of silence and humility,
you who are lost and found
in the mystery of the Lord.

You are availability and receptivity.
You are fertility and plenitude.
You are attention and tender care
towards all.
You are clothed in fortitude.

Human maturity
and spiritual elegance are alive in you.
You are your own mistress
before being our lady.

There is no dispersal in you.
In a simple and total act
your motionless soul is
identified with the Lord.
You are in God and God is in you.
Total mystery encompasses
and penetrates you,
possesses, dwells and integrates
your whole being.

It seems as if everything
has remained motionless in you,
has been identified with you;
time, space, word,
music, silence, woman, God.
Everything in you seems
to have been assumed and deified.

No one has ever seen
much gentle human image
and no one will ever see on earth
woman so lovingly interceding.

Nevertheless, your silence is not absence
but presence.
You are lost in the Lord,
and at the same time,
attentive to all of us, as in Cana.

Never is communication so profound
as when no word is uttered
and never is silence as eloquent
as when nothing is said.

Make us understand that silence
is not lack of interest for others
but that you are a radiant source of energy
that unfolds,
and to overflow,
one must be filled.

The world drowns
in the sea of dispersion,
and it is impossible to love one's brethren
with a dispersed heart.
Make us understand that,
as apostles, we must love silence
but that silence
without acts of mercy is simply comfort.

Cover us with the cloak of your silence,
and give us the strength of your faith,
the heights of your hope,
the depth of your love.

Remain with those who stay,
and come with us who go.

Oh admirable Mother of silence!

61. Prayer in times of exhaustion

Mother, I come from the turmoil of life. I am
exhausted, body and soul.

It is hard to peacefully accept what happens
around us in a day of work and struggle...
The things in which we had put so much
hope betray us. People to whom we wish to
be kind, resist us. And those from whom we
seek help try to take advantage.

This is why I come to you, Mother, because deep inside me lives an insecure child. But close to you I feel strong and full of confidence. Only the thought of having a mother such as you, gives me courage. I feel that your arm supports me and that your hand guides me. I can thus continue on my way undisturbed.

Renew me totally so that I may see the beauty of life. Lift me so that I may walk without fear. Give me your hand so that I may always find my way. Bless me so that my presence in the world may be a sign of your blessing. Amen.

62. Lady of Eastertide

Lady of Eastertide,
Lady of Friday and of Sunday,
Lady of night and of morning,
Lady of silence and of the cross,
Lady of love and surrender,
Lady of the word received
and of the word pledged,
Lady of peace and of hope.

Lady of every departure,
because you are the Lady

of the "passage" or of "passover", hear us.
Today, we wish to "thank you".
Thank you our Lady for your "fiat",
for your entire availability as servant,
for your poverty and your silence,
for the suffering of your seven swords,
for the joy of all your departures
which brought peace to so many.
Thank you very much
because you have remained with us
in spite of time and distance.

Our Lady of reconciliation,
image and beginning of the church;
today we place in your
silent and accessible heart,
this pilgrim church of Easter.

A church essentially missionary,
leaven and soul of the society,
in which we live,
a prophetic church, proclamation
of the kingdom which is already here.

A church of authentic witnesses,
inserted in the history of men
as the saving presence of the Lord,
source of peace, of joy and of hope. Amen.

63. Praise to God

You alone are holy, Lord God,
you who do wonders.
You are strong, you are great,
you are most high,
you are good, all good, supreme good,
Lord God, living and true.
You are charity and love, you are wisdom.
You are humility, you are patience,
you are protection,
you are peacefulness, you are well-being,
you are joy,
you are beauty, you are meekness.
You are our protector,
our guardian and our defensor.
You are our strength and our hope.
You are our sweetness.
You are our eternal life,
great and admirable Lord.

64. New Psalm of Creation
   (*Fragments*)

Allow us to praise you, Oh God,
in all the worlds you have created.

Allow us to praise you,
on the heights where angels abide.

Allow us to praise you
in the depths of the glistening stars.

Allow us to praise you, our God,
at the foot of the angel who closes hell.

Allow us to praise you, Oh God,
with the twittering birds,
noisy and multicolored
that rejoice eye and ear.

Allow us to praise you, Oh God,
for nests in the trees,
where fledglings lift
their bare necks
towards their mother bringing food.

Allow us to praise you, Oh God,
with mighty birds,
that fly over the seas,
and take wing towards
perpetual snows.

Allow us to praise you, Oh God,
for the animals of the earth,
big and small, full of tenderness,
or overflowing with untameable force.
Do not allow them to be extinguished
but let them live.

And may new generations come
also to praise you.

Allow us to praise you,
oh God, Trinity in one
for the animals of the earth
of nimble feet
and most pleasant to behold.
Do not let them perish
on account of animals
great and powerful, that crush everything,
for the large animal
also has a heart,
and little ones to protect.

Allow us to praise you
in the roundness of the earth
for everything that flies and runs,
swims and arises from the deep.

All things belong to you:
your finger is everywhere
pouring out beauty
in multicolored feathers;
it puts strength in winds
and in claws...

Your love is everywhere
unfathomable and impenetrable.

Everywhere small animals are born,
defenseless and blind,
seeking their mother's milk.

Blessed are you, One God and Trinity
for the splendid rocks
of mountains and glaciers.

Blessed are you for cascades
and mighty rivers,
for calm waters,
deep and silent.
Be praised with much affection
for small springs
that give water so that fish may live.

Praised are you, my God,
for storms
on earth and sea,
for sand storms
in the deserts.

Blessed are you, glorious God
for the splendor of millions
of scented flowers of beautiful forms.
This blossoming is unending
and will never be annihilated.
And even if you send a disaster
on a land, it never lasts long;
and a new spring arises;

and a new magnificence
governs the earth.

Allow us to praise you, Oh God,
for your angels.
They are powerful and admirable to behold.
They are servants of your will,
they combat for your word,
and humbly submit themselves
to your command.

Wonderful and eternal is your holy desire
to edify man more and more.
And even if he fails,
if he kneels before you
like a prodigal son,
you bend over him
with patience and kindness
telling him: Come child,
return to original innocence
and I shall welcome you
as a father greets his child.

Your patience towards men is immense,
oh God, eternal and excellent.

Nonetheless, man does not see it;
he invades fields, tramples flowers,
hunts birds and destroys nests.

A man fights another,
enslaves him,

imprisons him
and condemns him to death.

No one has such patience as you, my God,
and eternal praise addressed to you
will never cease on earth.
Allow us to adore you, eternally.
Let eternal praise
endure on earth.
As far as we reach to see,
all is yours, everything belongs to you,
your hand is upon every creature.

Be glorified and praised,
most holy God,
in each heart you created for your glory.
You want to be eternally with us,
most holy God.
You three times holy, praiseworthy,
you, our beatitude,
Oh three times holy,
three times admirable,
three times divine, ineffable God. Amen.

65. Face to Face

Day after day, Lord of my life,
may I remain before you,
face to face.

With clasped hands, I will stay before you,
Lord of all worlds,
face to face.

In this world that is yours,
in the midst of exhaustion,
turmoil, conflict,
of impassioned multitudes,
I must remain before you,
face to face.

And when my duty in this world
is achieved,
oh king of kings, alone and silent,
I will remain before you,
face to face. Amen.

TO PRAY

I. PRELIMINARY EXERCISES

Many people do not progress on the path of prayer because they overlook the necessary preparation.

At times, when you wish to pray, you will feel calm. In this case, there is no need to prepare yourself. Just concentrate, invoke the Holy Spirit, and pray.

On other occasions, as you begin to pray, you will feel so nervous and your thoughts so scattered that if you do not first calm down, you will not get anywhere.

And again, something else might occur, after many minutes of pleasant prayer, you find that you are getting tense and preoccupied. If at this particular moment you do not practice some relaxation exercise, not only will you waste time, but this period will prove unpleasant and counter-productive.

Here are a few easy exercises, it is up to you to decide which one to use, when, how much time and in what manner to use them: this all depends on need and circumstances.

When you wish to pray, always take a correct body position, head and trunk erect. Make sure you can breathe easily. Relax tensions and nerves, let go of memories and images, empty yourself and be silent. Concentrate. Place yourself in the presence of God, invoke the Holy Spirit and begin to pray. Four or five minutes of preparation are sufficient, that is, when you are normally calm.

Physical Relaxation. Calm and concentrating, release all tension in your legs and arms by stretching and contracting the muscles, feel how energy escapes. Loosen your shoulders in a similar manner; loosen the muscles of your face and forehead. Relax, close your eyes. Loosen the muscles and nerves in your neck by gently moving your head to and fro and turning it slowly from one side to the other, calmly and attentively. Feel how muscles and nerves relax. Take about ten minutes for this exercise.

Mental Relaxation. In a very calm and concentrated manner, start to repeat the word "peace" in a low voice — if possible when exhaling — and feel how a soothing peace first floods your brain — take a few minutes to feel how the brain relaxes and after this, go through your whole body, repeating the word "peace" and let yourself be flooded with a pleasant sensation of profound peace.

Afterward, repeat this same exercise with the word "nothing" and feel the sensation of *emptiness-nothing*, first in your brain and then through your whole being until you feel a general sensation of rest and silence. Take ten to fifteen minutes for this exercise.

Concentration. Calmly, detect the movement of your lungs — simply feel it and continue without thinking about anything. Concentrate on this for about five minutes.

After this, stay calm, quiet and attentive; notice and release from your attention all noises: far, near, strong or soft. About five minutes.

Following this, with great calm and attention, take your heartbeat, and concentrate on it, simply feeling the beats, without thinking about anything. About five minutes.

Respiration. Relax and be calm. Follow attentively what you are doing: inhale slowly through the nose until your lungs are filled, and expire through your mouth, slightly opened, until all the air is out. In short: a calm, slow and deep breathing.

The most relaxing breathing is abdominal: lungs are filled as the abdomen swells, they are emptied as the abdomen flattens. All this is simultaneous. Do not force anything: at first, do about ten respirations. With time, you will be able to add more.

You must use these exercises freely and with flexibility as far as time, occasion, etc. are concerned.

At the beginning, you might not feel results. But things will gradually improve. At such times, effects will be surprisingly positive. On other occasions, it will be the contrary. Such is our unpredictable nature.

Some people say prayer is a grace and does not depend on methods or exercises. This is a serious error. Life with God is a convergence between grace and nature. Prayer is a grace, yes; but it is also an art, and as such, it needs training, method and pedagogy. If many people are blocked in spiritual mediocrity, it is not because grace fails but due to lack of order, discipline and patience; in a word, because nature fails.

II. PRACTICAL GUIDELINES

1. If you feel sleepy when you pray, stand up, body straight and heels together.

2. When you experience aridity, think that this may be a test from God or an emergency of nature. Do not force yourself to "feel". Have the three angels accompany you: *Patience*: accept peacefully what you cannot resolve. *Perseverance:* continue to pray even though you may not feel anything. *Hope:* everything has an end, tomorrow will be better.

3. Never forget that life with God is a *life of faith*. And faith has nothing to do with feeling but with *knowledge*. It is not emotion but conviction. It is not evidence but certainty.

4. In order to pray, method, order, discipline and flexibility are needed, for the Holy Spirit blows when least expected. People stagnate in prayer because they lack method. He who prays without care becomes a careless person.

5. Do not dream, hope. A dream vanishes; hope endures. Effort, yes; violence, no. An intense struggle to feel devotion produces mental fatigue and discouragement.

6. Remember that God is gratuity. For this reason, his way of teaching us is bewildering; and for this very reason, there is no human logic to prayer; this particular effort should produce these results; this action, this reaction; this cause, this effect. On the contrary, there will usually be no proportion between your efforts in prayer and the "results". This is the way it is and it should be accepted peacefully.

7. Prayer is a relationship with God. Relationship is the movement of mental energies, a movement of adhesion to God. It is therefore normal that emotion or enthusiasm fill the soul. But beware! It is vital that this emotional state stays under the control of calm and serenity.

8. Divine visitation, when one prays, can occur at any moment: at the beginning, in the middle or at the end; at any moment or never. In this last case, be careful not to be taken over by discour-

agement and impatience. On the contrary, relax your nerves, abandon yourself, and continue to pray.

9. You complain: "I pray but it is not noticeable in my life." To receive strength from prayer in life, *first*: synthesize your morning prayer in a sentence — for example: "What would Jesus do in my place?" and recall it in each circumstance of the day. *Secondly*: when you experience a setback or a strong ordeal comes, be aware and remember that you have to feel and act like Jesus would.

10. Do not attempt to change your life; it will be enough to improve it. Do not try to be humble; it will suffice to do humble deeds. Do not endeavor to be virtuous; it is sufficient to perform deeds of virtue. To be virtuous is to act like Jesus.

Do not be frightened by relapse. Backsliding means that you act according to your negative features. Whenever you are careless or taken by surprise, you will react according to your negative impulses. This is normal. Be patient. When something comes up, try not to be taken off guard, be watchful and try to act according to the impulses of Jesus.

11. Be aware that you are capable of very little. I tell you this to encourage you, so that you will not lose heart due to any backsliding. Remember that to grow in God is extremely slow and full of countermarches. Accept this in peace. After each relapse, get up and go.

12. Holiness is to be with the Lord, and to be so much with him that his image is engraved in the soul; and to walk in the light of this image. This is holiness.

13. To take the first steps in your relationship with God, while you learn to pray, you may use guidelines 1, 2 and 3, suggested under "Methods" in the following section.

In the worst moments of dispersion or aridity, do not waste your time; you can always pray with the methods of written prayer, auditive prayer and prayed reading, which follow.

III. METHODS

1. Prayed Reading

Take a written prayer, for example a psalm or any other prayer, but be careful: this has nothing to do with reading one chapter of the Bible or a theme of meditation. The aim is to pray.

Take a prayerful body posture and an interior praying attitude. Calm yourself and invoke the Holy Spirit.

Begin to read the prayer slowly, very slowly. While reading, try to *experience* what you read. What I mean is that you try *to assume* the meaning of the words you read, to feel "with all your soul" making "yours" the sentences read, concentrating your attention on the content of the meaning of the sentences.

If you find an expression that you feel has much significance, stop immediately. Repeat it many times, and through it, unite yourself to the Lord until the richness of the phrase is depleted, or until its content floods your soul. Think that God is like the other shore; in order to be linked to this shore, many bridges are not necessary: one is enough. A sole sentence can keep us bound together.

If this does not happen, continue to read very slowly, assume and feel with your heart the meaning of what you read. Stop once in a while. Go back to repeat and relive the most significant expressions.

If at one point you sense that you can abandon the support of the reading, leave it aside and let the Holy Spirit fill your inner self with spontaneous and inspired thoughts.

This method is always easy and effective. It helps in a very particular way to take the first steps when one experiences aridity, or simply on those days when one cannot think of anything in particular because of mental dispersion or nervousness.

2. Meditated reading

One must carefully choose a book that does not disperse but rather concentrates, most preferably, the Bible. It is good to have a personal knowledge of it, that is, to know where to find themes that are significant to you — for example, on consolation, hope, patience, in order to choose among this material what your soul needs on this day in particular. You may also follow the liturgical order, with the help of texts proposed for each day.

It is not recommended to pen the Bible at random, or to do so very seldom. In any case, it is better to know, before the beginning of a meditated reading, what themes you wish to meditate and in which chapter of the Bible.

Take a correct position. Ask the assistance of the Holy Spirit and calm yourself.

Begin to read slowly, very slowly. As you read, try to *understand* what is read: the meaning of the sentence, its context, and the intention of the sacred author. Here lies the difference between a prayed reading and a meditated reading: in a prayed reading one *takes on and lives* what is read — this is fundamentally the task of the heart. In the meditated reading, one tries to *understand* what is read — this is basically an intellectual activity, since one handles concepts: explaining, applying, comparing them in order to go deeper within divine life, to develop principles of life, standards of judgment, in other words, a Christian mentality.

Continue to read slowly, in order to comprehend what you read.

If you find an idea which strikes your attention, stop right there; close the book; consider the idea in all ways possible; apply it to your life; draw conclusions.

If this does not happen — or after it did happen, continue to read in a peaceful concentrated and quiet manner.

If one paragraph seems difficult to understand, go back; try to read enough to grasp the meaning; understand this particular passage in the broader context.

Continue to read slowly and attentively.

If at some point your heart is moved and you are prompted to praise, give thanks or implore... feel free to do so.

If nothing happens, continue to read slowly, understanding and considering what you read.

It is normal and convenient for a meditated reading to end in prayer. Try to do this.

Through meditated reading, it is desirable to reach practical criteria to be implemented in one's daily living.

We strongly suggest that during meditation you always hold a book in your hands, especially the Bible, otherwise much time is lost, although it is not necessary to read during the entire period. Saint Theresa tells us that for fourteen years she was unable to meditate unless she held a book in her hands.

3. Concise instructions to meditate and live the Word

1. Read slowly, very slowly, pausing frequently.

2. Keep your soul empty, open and expectant.

3. Read unselfishly: do not try to find something, like doctrine, truths...

4. Read, "listening" to the Lord heart to heart, person to person, attentively, but with a "passive" attention, without anxiety.

5. Do not constrain yourself to *understand* intellectually nor literally. Do not be preoccupied with knowing "what does *this* mean" but ask yourself "what is God telling me by this?" Do not take time on detached sentences that, in some cases, do not bear any meaning by themselves. Drop them, do not be preoccupied with understanding everything literally.

6. If an expression strikes you, underline it and write in the margin a word that summarizes this strong impression.

7. Remove names — for example Israel, Jacob, Samuel, Moses, Timothy... and put yours in its place. Feel how God calls you by name.

8. If the reading does not "say" anything to you, stay untroubled, peaceful. It may well be that another day the same reading will "say" much; for along with our work there is, or there is not, grace; God's time is not our time, you must always have much patience in the things of God.

9. Do not struggle to catch and possess the exact doctrinal meaning of the Word, but meditate it like Mary did, ruminate it in your mind and heart, let it fill you and become saturated with the vibrations and echoes of God's heart, and "keep" the Word, that is, let it echo throughout the whole day.

10. In the psalms, "imagine" what Jesus or Mary felt while pronouncing the same words; place yourself mentally in the heart of Jesus Christ and say these words to God, as Jesus might have, pray them in his spirit, with his inner disposition, with his feelings.

11. Put the meditated work frequently into practice in your life: reflect upon what feelings and circumstances the criteria included in the Word — God's *mind* must influence and alter our ways of thinking and behaving, for the Word must question the life of the believer; in this manner, God's criteria will become ours until we become transformed into real disciples of the Lord.

12. In summary: read, savor, ponder, meditate and practice the Word.

4. Auditive exercise

Take a powerful expression that fills your soul — for example "my God and my all" — or a simple word, for example "Jesus", "Lord", "Father".

Begin to utter it, peacefully and deliberately, in low voice, every ten or fifteen seconds.

As you say it, try to experience the content of the word. Feel that the content is the Lord himself.

Begin to perceive how the "presence" or "substance" contained in this expression slowly and gently inundates your whole being and your mental energies.

Continue to repeat the expression slowly leaving more and more silence in between each repetition.

You must always use the same expression.

Variant: When we inhale, our body becomes tense because the lungs fill. On the contrary, when we exhale, our body relaxes, lets go.

In this variation, take advantage of the exhalation — natural moment of relaxation — to pronounce these expressions. Thus, both body and soul function in harmony. Concentration is easier, since respiration and blood irrigation are excellent. Results are supremely beneficial to the soul as well as to the body.

5. Written prayer

In this prayer, one writes what he or she would like to say to the Lord.

This may well be the only way to pray in times of emergency, in moments of deep aridity or of acute dispersion, on days when one feels desperate or annoyed.

One of the advantages of this method is to deeply concentrate our attention; it also has the advantage of being useful in future moments of prayer, as you read your own writings.

6. Visual exercise

One takes an expressive picture, for example an image of Jesus, of Mary or any other subject, a picture that makes a strong impression, such as peace, gentleness, strength... What is important is that it speaks to you deeply.

Take the picture in your hands and after calming down and invoking the Holy Spirit, stay quiet simply looking at the picture, first as a whole, then in detail.

Secondly, capture intuitively, attentively and with serenity the impressions this picture evokes in you. What does this image tell you?

Thirdly, with much calmness, transfer yourself to the picture, as if you were this image, or as if you were in it. Respectfully and calmly make "yours" the impressions this picture arouses in you. Thus, identify yourself mentally with this image, remain so for a good while, and saturate your soul with the sentiments of Jesus which the picture illustrates. This is how the soul puts on the image of Jesus and shares in his interior disposition.

Finally with this inner disposition, transfer yourself mentally to your daily life, imagine difficult situations and overcome them with Jesus' attitudes. This is the way to become an image of Jesus in the world.

This exercise is particularly fruitful for those who are naturally imaginative.

7. Prayer of Self-Surrender

This prayer — and attitude — is the truest to the Gospel. The most liberating. The most appeasing. No anaesthetic can ease life's sorrows better than to say "I surrender myself unto you, Lord."

We recommend that you memorize prayer number 35 in this book, and say it as you do "The Lord's Prayer" when you encounter every day obstacles, big or small.

Put yourself in an attitude of dedication, in the presence of the Father who allows or permits everything. You may use prayer number 35 to express yourself, or a simpler one such as: *your will be done, in your hands I commend myself.*

It is crucial to completely silence your mind which tends to rebel. Self-surrender is homage of silence in faith.

Place in silence and peace, with a prayer, everything that annoys you: your parents, your bodily features, illnesses, old age, powerlessness and limitations, negative traits of your personality, persons close to you who upset you, unhappy memories, painful experiences, failures, errors...

It might well be that when you remember them they will hurt. But if you place them in the hands of the Father, peace will enfold you.

8. Exercise of Acceptance

As in exercise No. 9 "Elevation", where we come out and peacefully await, the "I" goes out and settles in the "You"; in this exercise of acceptance, I remain quiet and receptive, and the YOU comes out to me and I joyfully greet his coming. It is convenient to do this exercise with the resurrected Christ.

We will use the verb *to feel*, not in the sense of being moved, but rather of *perceiving*. Much can be felt without being moved. I feel the cold ground, I feel a headache, I feel it is hot, I feel sad with no particular emotion.

With the help of certain phrases — which I will indicate at the end, in faith, begin to welcome Jesus who rose to life and who makes you rise to life, he who comes to you. Let the Spirit of Jesus come into you and fill your life. Feel the resurrected presence of Jesus come into the most hidden corners of your soul while you enunciate the phrases at the end of this exercise. Feel how this presence takes full possession of what you are, of what you think, of what you do, feel how Jesus takes over your innermost heart. In faith, welcome him without restraint, joyfully.

In faith, feel how Jesus touches that wound that so hurts you; feel how Jesus takes away the thorn of this oppressing anguish; sense how he relieves you from these fears, he liberates you of resentments. You must notice that these sensations are generally felt in the stomach, as a jab. This is why one speaks of a sword of pain.

After this, leap into life. Accompanied by Jesus and clothed in his likeness, stroll mentally along the places where you live or work. Stand before someone with whom you have clashes. Imagine how Jesus would look at that person. Look at him with the eyes of Jesus. Imagine Jesus' serenity if he had to face this conflict or confront this situation. Imagine all sorts of situations, even the most difficult ones, and let Jesus act through you: look with the eyes of Jesus, speak through his mouth. Let his appearance be your appearance. It is not you who live but Jesus who lives in you.

This is a transforming or "christifying" exercise.

Take a prayerful position, the same as in the exercise *Departure and Tranquillity*. After having vocalized and lived the phrase, remain still and silent for a while, let the meaning of these words resound and fill all your soul.

Jesus, come within me.
Take possession of my whole being.
Take me with all that I am,
what I think, what I do.

Take the most intimate part of my heart.
Cure this wound that hurts me so.
Take away the thorn of this anguish.

Remove from me this fear,
this resentment, these temptations...

Jesus, what do you want of me?
How would you look at this person?
What would be your attitude
in this particular difficulty?
How would you behave in this situation?
May those who see me see you, Jesus.
Transform me totally into you.
May I become a living transparency
of your person.

This exercise must last
from forty-five to fifty minutes.

9. Departure and Tranquillity

In this exercise, one pronounces mentally or
in low voice an expression — that I will
indicate later.

Motivated by the phrase, the "I" goes out
towards the YOU. When you take and live
the meaning of the expression, it captures
your attention, carries it and lays it on a
YOU. There is thus a movement or departure. In this manner, the whole "I" remains
in the whole YOU.

Stay calm, motionless. There is also a still-ness.

Here is what I mean: there must not be any mental movement. You must not be preoc-cupied with the *meaning* of the phrase. In all understanding there is a coming and going. As for ourselves, we are now in adoration. Therefore, there must not be any analytical activity.

On the contrary: the mind, prompted by the phrase, goes forth towards a YOU, silent and clinging admiringly, contemplatively, possessively, lovingly. For example, if you say "You are the immutable eternity", you must not preoccupy yourself with under-standing or analyzing how and why God is eternal, but look at him and admire him passively as eternal.

After silencing your whole being, in faith become aware of the presence of the One in whom we exist, move and are.

Begin to utter the sentence in low voice. Try to live what the sentence says until your soul becomes saturated with the substance of the phrase.

After you have said it, remain in silence about thirty seconds or more, quiet, still as one who listens to an echo. The attention is motionless, possessively absorbed, identified to the substance of the phrase; that is, to God himself.

In this exercise you must let yourself be seized by the YOU. The "I" practically disappears while the YOU controls the whole sphere.

Here are some expressions that may be used in this exercise.

You are my God.
For ever and ever you are God.
You are motionless eternity.
You are infinite immensity.
You are without beginning or end.
You are so far and so close.
You are my all.
Oh depth of the essence
and presence of my God!

You are my total rest.
Only in you do I feel peace.
You are my strength.
You are my security.
You are my patience.
You are my joy.
You are my eternal life,
great and marvellous Lord.

10. "In Place of" Jesus

Imagine Jesus in adoration, at night, under the stars, or in the early morning.

With infinite reverence, in faith and peace, penetrate the heart of Jesus. Try to observe and revive what Jesus experienced in his relationship with the Father, and you will thus participate in the profound experience of the Lord.

Try to scrutinize and revive the feelings of admiration Jesus had towards the Father. Say with the heart of Jesus, with his vibrations, for example, "glorify your name", "hallowed be your name."

Install yourself in the heart of Jesus, take on his harmonics and revitalize the attitude of self-surrender and of submission he experienced in the face of the Father's will when he said: "Let your will be done, not mine." "Your will be done."

Try to experience what he felt when he said "for You and I are one," when he uttered "Abba" — dear Father! Place yourself in the heart of Jesus to say the priestly prayer, Chapter 17 of the Gospel according to Saint John.

In faith make these — and so many more things "yours" in the Spirit, in order to be clad with the inner disposition of Jesus. And come back into everyday life carrying the profound life of Jesus.

This prayer will only be possible through the Holy Spirit, "who teaches the whole truth."

11. Prayer of contemplation

According to Saint John of the Cross, the signs that a soul has entered contemplation are the following:

— The soul likes to be alone, in loving and quiet attention with God.

— Even if one seems to be wasting time, the soul is left quiet and calm, attentive to God, in an inner peace, and rest.

— The soul is left free from preoccupation without thinking or meditating; only a sustained and loving concentration of God.

a) *Silence.* Empty yourself spiritually. Suspend all activity of the senses. Silence memories. Unbind preoccupations.

Isolate yourself from both the outside and the inside world. Do not think about anything. Better still, do not think anything.

Stay beyond feeling and action, do not concentrate on anything, do not look at anything, either internally or externally.

Outside of me, nothing; inside of me, nothing.

What is left? An attention of myself on myself, in silence and peace.

b) *Presence.* To open one's attention on the Other, in faith, as when one looks without thinking, as one who loves and feels loved.

Avoid imagining God. All images or forms of God must disappear. It is better "to silence" any notion of location of God. The verb that corresponds to God is the verb *to be.*

He *is* the pure, loving, surrounding, penetrating and omnipresent presence.

There only remains a You towards which I am an open, loving and peaceful attention.

Practice the auditive exercise until the word "falls" by itself. Remain without uttering anything with your lips, nothing with your mind.

To look and feel that you are being seen.
To Love and feel loved.
I am like a beach. He is like the sea.
I am like a meadow. He is like the sun.
Let yourself be enlightened,
inundated, LOVED.
LET YOURSELF BE LOVED.

Formula for the exercise:

You analyze me.
You know me.
You love me.

12. To pray with nature

If the person is outdoors, facing a splendid landscape, one of the methods of prayer he can use is to pray with nature.

Start with the prayed reading of Psalm 104. In the spirit of this Psalm, begin to contemplate, look at, admire all that your eyes see.

Continue to admire, being impressed by each and every one of the creatures that parade by in the Psalm: clouds, winds, snow covered peaks, cascades, rivers, valleys, springs, birds, nests, streams, refreshing vales, plants, butterflies, flowers, grain, olives, vineyards, age-old trees, minute grass blades, sun, moon, light, shadow...

For each creature contemplated and admired, say: "My God, how great you are." (v. 1).

Once in a while, repeat verse 24: "How countless are your works, Lord, all of them made so wisely! The earth is full of your creatures".

Listen, absorb and submerge yourself in the harmony of the whole creation. Keep yourself concentrated and receptively attentive to each one of the voices of the world: thousands of insects that sing out their joy of living, the varied sound of so many birds; the murmur of the wind or of the river; crickets, frogs, roosters, dogs, all living beings that express their joy of living and, in their own way, acclaim and sing gratefully to their Lord. In their name and with them, say: "All creatures of the Lord, bless the Lord."

Arouse in yourself a sensation of universal brotherhood: feel, in God, that each creature is your brother, your sister, feel that in God you are one with all that your eyes see; submerge yourself vitally in the great family of creation, without being conscious of it, feel yourself a joyous part of the happiness to live what each of them experience, as if you swam in the sea of universal life and vibrated with the tenderness of the world.

Implore their forgiveness for being enslaved by man; for being trampled so often and for being treated with cruelty. Feel and express gratitude for all the benefits creatures contribute to the bliss of man.

Enter in a close dialogue with one particular creature: a flower, a tree, a stone, water from a stream. Question it about its origin, its history, its health, and listen to it attentively. In an intimate dialogue, recall to it your own history. Admire it and thank it for its beauty, its perfume, its contribution to the world harmony. Enter into a friendly climate with this creature.

During this long *prayer with nature*, frequently insert verses 1, 24, 31, 33 of Psalm 104 — always kept open in your hands, and also Psalm 8, especially the first refrain: "Lord, our God, how majestic is your name throughout the world".

13. Community prayer

Community Prayer, also called *shared*, is when a group gets together to pray, and it does so in the following manner: a) spontaneously; b) aloud; c) before each other; d) alternating individually — not everyone at the same time.

In order that community — or shared — prayer be really effective and convincing, the following conditions are compulsory:

1. One assumes that the people who share prayer have previously intensified a personal relationship with the Lord. Otherwise, community prayer becomes an artificial and empty activity.

2. Each person must avoid, as much as possible, repetition of short sentences, stereotypes, or formal expressions said from memory.

On the contrary, one must pray spontaneously, from the heart, as if at this particular moment you were alone in the world with Him. Pray informally, naturally.

3. To do this, those who pray must be convinced and must remember that they carry great inner riches, more precious than they can imagine, that the Holy Spirit lives within them, and that he expresses himself through their mouth; this is why they must speak with much ease and freedom.

4. It is to be expected that no emotional short circuit exists among those who pray. For if between two persons or groups there is a strong disagreement, well-known and public, this conflict hinders the spontaneity of the group. The walls that separate one brother from another also separate the brother from God.

5. It is also indispensable that sincerity and truth exist; that is to say, that the one who prays, when expressing himself verbally, is not motivated by pride to utter original or brilliant things. He must at all times rectify his intention,

and express himself as if he were alone before God.

6. But the essential condition is that prayer is truly *shared*: when a member of the group speaks with the Lord, I must not only be one who hears or an observer but — it is implied — that I take on the words that come out of my brother's mouth, and with these same words I address myself to my God. And when I vocalize my prayer, it is implied that my brothers take my words, and with these same words, address themselves to God. In this manner, *each one* prays *with each other* all the time. Here is the secret of the grandeur and richness of community prayer: the Holy spirit overflows through such diverse personalities and histories; this is why the result is a very enriching prayer.

14. Community Meditation

Community or shared meditation occurs when various people get together to take the Word of God or another theme, and to express spontaneously before the others what this theme or word suggests to them.

In order that community meditation be truly effective and convincing, the conditions detailed for community prayer must be taken into consideration, especially numbers 3, 4 and 5.

Moreover, to acclimatize oneself, it is advisable to begin with an invocation to the Holy Spirit, and with a brief and spontaneous prayer or a psalm.

It is also advisable to start the meditation by reading a portion of the Bible or of any other book, in order to circumscribe the subject of the meditation and to shed light on the theme.

It is very convenient that throughout the reflection one refers and makes application to life, determining practical standards so that these criteria may become concrete decisions for fraternal life or pastoral activity.

15. Variants

a) *Community prayer based on Psalms*

In this prayer, each person has in front of him a given Psalm. The group first reads it slowly together; next, each one prays it privately, in silence, following the method *Prayed reading*.

After two minutes, any one prays out loud — always holding the open psalm in his hand, making some kind of paraphrase or comment on the verse that most attracted his attention. Afterward, another does the same. And so on for all who wish to take part. End with a song.

b) *Community meditation based on the Word*

This is somewhat similar to the preceding. Each one holds the Bible open at a particular chapter, and one from the group reads an excerpt. All remain silent while each person meditates privately, always holding the open Bible.

After this, any one from the group comments — in the form of a reflection — the verse that most struck him. Next, another does the same, and successively all who wish. End with a song.

16. Meditation

This spiritual activity is recommended for people who have an analytical mind. For them, it is not sufficient to only meditate a reading, but they can and should advance deeper.

We must not forget that the great figures of God are formed in meditation.

To meditate is a mental activity, concentrated and arranged, by which we take a text or a theme, and we go along to contemplate it as a whole and in its details. We analyze it in its causes and its effects in order to consider life criteria, value judgments, in other words, a mentality according to God's mind. In this way, criteria become convictions and convictions become decisions. In this manner we are converted into *disciples of the Lord.*

To Prepare

— Pray for light;
— Choose the matter that will be meditated;
— In order to help the mind concentrate, it is advisable to imagine the scene graphically: what are they talking about, how do they move, the setting, other details.

To unravel and to put in order

— Distinguish the different levels of a scene; look for the meaning and the purpose of each word and for the context of the words, the meaning of each scene and the context of the scene; linger on the significance of the verbs...

— Infer, deduce, explain, implement, combine different ideas, compare them...

— Look for the internal logic of cause and effect, principles and conclusions, what each thing is and what it is not, distinguish the reasons and the intentions, action and reaction, effort and result.

To apply or to get involved

— I must *place myself* in the scene, as if I were an actor and not an observer: they speak to me and they question me — the words of Christ to Zacchaeus, Peter, the rich young man, the blind man on the road... are addressed to me — and I, in turn, talk, question these persons in the scene...

- — I Compare what I hear in the scene with my problems of today, with my present situation, the events of our times...

- — I end with a prayer.

IV. PROBLEMS OF FORGIVENESS

We are very seldom offended; we very often feel offended.

To forgive is to abandon or to eliminate an adverse feeling against our brother.

Who suffers? The one who hates or the one who is hated? The person hated generally lives happily in this world. The one who cultivates resentment is like one who seizes a live coal or who stirs up a flame. It would seem that the flame would burn the enemy; but no, it burns him. Resentment destroys only the resentful.

Pride is blind and suicidal: it prefers the satisfaction of vengeance to the relief of forgiveness. But to hate is absurd: it is like stocking up venom in one's entrails. The resentful person lives in perpetual agony.

In the whole world the most delicious fruit is the sensation of rest and relief felt when forgiving, and there is no fatigue as unpleasant as the one produced by resentment. It is really worthwhile to forgive, even if only out of personal interest, since no other therapy is more liberating than forgiveness.

It is not necessary to ask forgiveness or to forgive with words. Many times a greeting, a kind look, a conversation, or to get closer is sufficient. These are the best signs of forgiveness.

Sometimes this will occur: people forgive and feel the forgiveness; but after a while, aversion returns. Do not be surprised. A deep wound needs many healings. Forgive again and again until the wound is completely healed.

Exercises in forgiving

1. In faith, place yourself in the spirit of Jesus. Assume his feelings. Face the "enemy" — mentally —, look at him through Jesus' eyes, perceive him with Jesus' feelings, embrace him with Jesus' arms as if "you were" Jesus.

Concentrated, in full intimacy with the Lord Jesus — the "enemy" placed in the back of your memory, say to the Lord: Jesus, come within me. Take possession of my being.

Calm my hostilities. Give me your heart, poor and humble. I wish to feel towards this "enemy" what you feel towards him; what you felt when you died for him. Your feelings highly united to mine, I forgive — with you, I love, I embrace this person, He or She-You-I, one same thing. I-You-He or She, one same unity.

Repeat these or similar words for about thirty minutes.

2. If we understood, we would never have to forgive. Bring the "enemy" back to your memory and apply the following thoughts to him.

Except in very rare cases, no one acts out of bad intention. Are you not ascribing to this person wicked intentions he never had? In the end, who is mistaken? If he makes you suffer, have you thought how much you make him suffer? Who knows if he really said what they told you he had said? Who knows if he said it with a different tone of voice, or in another context?

He seems proud; it is not pride, it is shyness. He seems stubborn; it is not obstinacy, it is a reflex of self-affirmation. His conduct seems aggressive towards you; it is not aggressive-

155

ness, it is self-defense, a way to secure himself. He does not attack you, he defends himself. And you presume his heart full of wickedness. Who is unjust and wrong?

Of course, you find him troublesome; he may be more so to himself. It is true you suffer because of his ways; he suffers much more himself. If there is one person on earth interested in not being thus, it is not you, it is he. He would like to please everyone; he cannot. He would like to live in peace with all; he cannot. He would like to be charming; he cannot. If he had chosen his ways, he would be the most gracious person in the world. Does it make sense for you to be irritated by a way of being he has not chosen? Is he as guilty as you suppose him to be? In the end, is it not you, with your assumptions and repulsions, who are more unjust than he?

If we understood, there would be no need to forgive.

3. This is an act of the mind by which we release the attention of the person who has become an enemy. You interrupt this link of attention — by which your mind was tied to

this person — and you remain disconnected from him, and in peace.

You are not to expel this person violently from your mind, because in this manner he would become more affixed. What happens here is that you suspend for a moment that mental activity, you make a mental vacuum, and the "enemy" disappears. He will come back. Once more, suspend your mental activity or turn your attention towards something else.

There are a few popular verbs that signify this forgiveness: *To untie:* the attention is tied down, untie. *To unfasten:* it is fastened, unfasten. *To let go:* the memory grasps, you let it go. *To abandon. To forget.*

As you see, this is not forgiveness as such, but it does have its effects. It might be the first step, especially for a recently suffered moral injury.

V. HOW TO LIVE
A DESERT

The only way to revitalize the things of God is by revitalizing the heart. When the heart is filled with God, the things of life are filled with the enchantment of God. And the heart is brought back to life during "Significant Moments." So did the prophets, the saints, and above all, Christ.

A "Significant Moment" is a time set aside to be with the Lord, bits of time in the daily activity program, for example thirty minutes a day; a few hours every two weeks, etc. "Significant Moments" are intended not only to pray but also to recuperate emotional balance, interior unity, serenity and peace; otherwise, people disintegrate in the insanity of life.

Those who wish to take their life with God seriously, need to include the system of "Significant Moments" in their schedule of activities. If you save "Significant Moments," "Significant Moments" will save you from the emptiness of life and of existential disappointment. If you complain that you have no time, I will tell you that time is a question of preference; and preferences depend on priorities. We have time for what we prefer.

When one whole day is dedicated to the Lord — at least seven hours — in silence and solitude, this day is called a *desert*.

In order to live a *desert*, it is advisable, almost necessary, to go out of the place one lives or works, and to withdraw in a solitary location, in the country, a forest, on a mountain or in a retreat house.

It is wise to live the *desert* in small groups, for example, three to five, but, once you have reached the location where you will spend the day, it is essential to disperse, and each person remain absolutely alone. In the last hours, you may come together to fraternally exchange experiences and pray as a community.

It is desirable that each person take along something to eat, while not forgetting that the *desert* also has a penitential nature. Nonetheless, you must not abstain from taking liquids in order to avoid dehydration.

In short: A *desert* is a time of retreat dedicated to God in silence, solitude and penance.

It is recommendable to have with you an assortment of biblical texts, psalms, exercises for relaxation — these are all found in this book. Do not forget to take along a notebook to jot down your impressions.

Guidelines

1. Use these guidelines with flexibility since the Holy Spirit may have other plans. You must allow leeway for the spontaneity of grace. For example, feel very free with the time schedule I give for each point.

2. Once you have reached the place where you will spend the day, begin with a prayed reading of psalms. This is to prepare a favorable atmosphere for the deeper spiritual level of the person. About sixty minutes.

3. If your thoughts feel scattered, prepare yourself with exercises for relaxation, concentration and silence. About thirty minutes. You may repeat these exercises all through the day; but from the very

beginning, you must achieve an elementary state of serenity.

4. Personal dialogue with the Lord God, not necessarily a dialogue of words but of inwardness, to talk with God, to be with Him, to love and to feel loved... This is the most important spiritual attitude of the *desert*. You may use the techniques described above. Around seventy five minutes.

5. Since this is a day of intense cerebral activity, it is good to have a few brief intervals of rest when the most important thing is to do nothing but rest.

6. A *desert* cannot be without a prolonged *meditated reading* following the method explained in the second technique. Use biblical texts, compare your personal and apostolic life with the Word of God. About eighty minutes.

7. There must also be a pleasant and lengthy dialogue with Jesus Christ, with him explicitly. Talk with him as a friend speaks to a friend, walk along with him, in your imagination, on the roads of life, solving difficulties. About fifty minutes.

8. An intense exercise of self-surrender; to heal the wounds again, to accept so many things that have been rejected, to forgive oneself and to forgive others, to strengthen peace. About forty minutes.

Have close at hand the practical guidelines given in this book. Do not become euphoric when consolation arises, nor depressed when aridity creeps in. The safest criteria of divine presence is peace. If you have peace, even in deep aridity, God is with you. Remember how many deserts lived Jesus.

Bible References for the Desert

To go to the desert is to go on a pilgrimage like the People of God who searched for the face of God.

Old Testament

Moses encounters God in the desert: Ex 3: 1-15.

God leads the People of Israel through the desert: Ex 14-20; 24; Nb 9:15-24.

The face of God leads Moses through the desert: Ex 33:7-23.

The steps of the desert: Nb 10-14; 16; 17; 20.

The desert, a place where God is manifest: Ex 19.

Elijah encounters God in the desert: 1K 19: 3-15.

The desert, a place of purification: Nb 20: 1-13.

New Testament

John, greatest of prophets, in the desert: Lk 1:13-17; 3:1-6; Mk 1:1-8; Mt 3:1-13.

Jesus man of the desert.

Thirty years of silence and anonymity: Lk 3:23.

Immediate preparation to his mission — lead to the desert: Lk 4:1-13; Mt 4:1-11; Mk 1:12.

Jesus withdraws in total solitude to be with the Father: Lk 6:12; Mt 14:13; Mk 6:46; Mt 14:23; Jn 6:15; Mk 7:24; Lk 9:10; Mk 1:35; Mt 6:6; Mk 14:32; Mt 17:1; Lk 9:28; Mt 26:26; Lk 22:39; Mk 9:2; Lk 3:21; Lk 4:1-13; Lk 9:18; Lk 21:37; Lk 4:42; Lk 5:1; Lk 11:1.

Paul spends three years in the desert: Ga 1:15-18.

John remains alone in his exile in Asia Minor: Rv 1:9f.

Bible Texts for Significant Moments

Psalms: 16, 23, 25, 27, 31, 36, 40, 42, 51, 56, 61, 62, 63, 69, 71, 77, 84, 86, 88, 90, 91, 93, 96, 103, 104, 118, 119, 123, 126, 130, 131, 139, 143.

(Please be aware that I use the numbering of the Hebrew Bible which is adopted by all our modern editions. Books of Divine Office follow the numbering of the *Vulgate* for which we have to subtract one.)

Magnificence of God: Is 2:9-23; 40:12-31; 41: 21-29; 44:1-9.

Prophetic Call: Jr 1:4-11; Is 49:1-7.

Apostolic Life: 1 Co 4:9-14; 2 Co 4:1-18; 2 Co 6:3-11; 2 Co 11:23-30.

Patience: Eccl. 2:1-7.

Compassion of God: Ho 2:16-25; Is 41:8-20; Os 11:1-6.

Irresistible faith: Rm 8:28-39.

Divine filiation: Rm 8:15-22.

Courage and Hope: Jos 1; Is 43; Is 54; Is 60.

Christ, Center of the World: Col 1:15-21; Ep 3:14-21.

Historical Texts: Ac 14-28; 2 Tm; 1 M chapters 2 to 5; 2 M chapters 5 to 8.

Jesus, merciful and compassionate: Mt 9:35; Mk 1:41; Mt 14:14; Lk 7:13; Mk 2:17; Mt 11:19; Mt 9:9; Lk 15:1f; Mt 9:13; Lk 7:36, Jn 8:1f.

Jesus, meek, patient and humble: Mk 3:10; Lk 5:1; Mt 5:5; Mk 14:56; Mt 27:13, Lk 23:8; Lk 23:24; Mt 4:1-11; 2 Co 10:1; 1 P 2:23.

Option of Jesus for the poor: Mt 9:36; Mk 6:34; Lk 6:20; Mt 11:5; Lk 4:18; Mt 25:34f.

Jesus, sincere and true: Mt 5:37; Mt 16:21; Lk 13:32; Jn 8:40f; Jn 6:66; Mt 7:3; Lk 7:39; Jn 8:32; Jn 18:37; 1 P 2:22.

To love as Jesus loved: Jn 13:34; Mt 19:14; Jn 11:1f; Jn 15:15; Jn 20:27; Mk 10:45; Mt 20:28; Jn 15:9; Jn 3:16; Ga 2:20.